Edward Albee was born in 1928, and began writing plays thirty years later. His previous plays are, in order of composition, *The Zoo Story* (1958); *The Death of Bessie Smith* (1959); *The Sandbox* (1959); *The American Dream* (1960); *Who's Afraid of Virginia Woolf?* (1961-1962); *The Ballad of the Sad Café*, adapted from Carson McCullers' novella (1963); *Tiny Alice* (1964); *Malcolm*, adapted from James Purdy's novel (1965); and *A Delicate Balance* (1966).

"Edward Albee is not merely our most hopeful playwright, our most promising playwright, our most interesting play-wright—he is, quite simply, our best play-wright."

—*The New York Times*

Everything in the Garden
was originally published by Atheneum.

Other books by Edward Albee

A Delicate Balance
Tiny Alice
Who's Afraid of Virginia Woolf?

Published by Pocket Books

*Are there paperbound books you want
but cannot find in your retail stores?*

You can get any title in print in:
Pocket Book editions • Pocket *Cardinal* editions • Permabook editions or Washington Square Press editions. Simply send retail price, local sales tax, if any, plus 15¢ to cover mailing and handling costs for each book wanted to:
MAIL SERVICE DEPARTMENT
    POCKET BOOKS • A Division of Simon & Schuster, Inc.
    1 West 39th Street • New York, New York 10018
    Please send check or money order. We cannot be responsible for cash.
    Catalogue sent free on request.

Titles in these series are also available at discounts in quantity lots for industrial or sales-promotional use. For details write our Special Projects Agency: The Benjamin Company, Inc., 485 Madison Avenue, New York, N.Y. 10022.

EVERYTHING IN THE GARDEN

A PLAY BY
EDWARD ALBEE

from the play by Giles Cooper

PUBLISHED BY POCKET BOOKS NEW YORK

EVERYTHING IN THE GARDEN

Atheneum edition published March, 1968

A Pocket Book edition
1st printing .... March, 1969

CAUTION: Professionals and amateurs are hereby warned that *Everything in the Garden,* being fully protected under the Copyright Laws of the United States of America, the British Empire, including the Dominion of Canada, and all other countries of the Berne and Universal Copyright Conventions, is subject to royalty. All rights, including professional, amateur, motion picture, recitation, lecturing, public reading, radio and television broadcasting, and the rights of translation into foreign languages, are strictly reserved. Particular emphasis is laid on the question of readings, permission for which must be secured from the author's agent in writing. All inquiries should be addressed to the William Morris Agency, 1350 Avenue of the Americas, New York, N. Y.

This *Pocket Book* edition includes every word contained in the original, higher-priced edition. It is printed from brand-new plates made from completely reset, clear, easy-to-read type. *Pocket Book* editions are published by Pocket Books, a division of Simon & Schuster, Inc., 630 Fifth Avenue, New York, N.Y. 10020. Trademarks registered in the United States and other countries.

Standard Book Number: 671-77063-2.
Library of Congress Catalog Card Number: 68-16862.
Copyright, ©, 1968, by Edward Albee. From the play
Everything in the Garden by Giles Cooper, copyright, ©, 1963, 1964, by Giles Cooper. All rights reserved. This **Pocket Book** edition is published by arrangement with Atheneum.

Printed in the U.S.A.

TO THE MEMORY OF
GILES COOPER

FIRST PERFORMANCE
November 16, 1967, New York City, Plymouth Theatre

BARBARA BEL GEDDES *as* JENNY

BARRY NELSON *as* RICHARD

ROBERT MOORE *as* JACK

BEATRICE STRAIGHT *as* MRS. TOOTHE

RICHARD THOMAS *as* ROGER

MARY K. WELLS *as* BERYL

WHITFIELD CONNOR *as* CHUCK

M'EL DOWD *as* LOUISE

TOM ALDREDGE *as* GILBERT

CHARLES BAXTER *as* PERRY

AUGUSTA DABNEY *as* CYNTHIA

Directed by PETER GLENVILLE

THE PLAYERS

RICHARD
a pleasant-looking man, 43

JENNY
his wife, an attractive woman in her late thirties

ROGER
their son, a nice-looking boy, 14 or 15

JACK
a neighbor, a pleasant-looking man, about 40

MRS. TOOTHE
an elegantly dressed, handsome lady, 50 or so

CHUCK AND BERYL

GILBERT AND LOUISE

CYNTHIA AND PERRY
friends and neighbors,
very much like Richard and Jenny

THE SCENE

The livingroom and sunroom of a suburban house, a large and well-kept garden visible through the glass doors of the sunroom. This was an old house and the sunroom is clearly an addition to the existing structure, though not jarring. There is no wealth evident in the set; taste and ingenuity have been used instead of money.

ACT ONE

SCENE ONE

(Stage empty, sounds of lawnmower (hand) out picture window. RICHARD *passes window, mowing; stops, mops; goes on.* JENNY *enters room from hall, looking for a cigarette; finds pack on mantel, finds it empty, is about to throw it away, remembers, removes coupons, then is about to throw pack in wastebasket when she spies another empty pack therein, shakes her head, stoops, takes it out, un-crumples it, removes coupons)*

JENNY
(Shakes her head; under her breath)
Honestly! *(Louder, but* RICHARD *cannot possibly hear)*
You might remember!
*(*RICHARD *passes window again, mowing;* JENNY
opens glass door, speaks out to him)*
You might remember!
(He goes on mowing; irritated)
Richard!
(He stops)

RICHARD
(We really don't hear him)
Hm?

JENNY
You might try to remember! *(Turns, comes back in, leaving glass door open)*

3

RICHARD
(Follows her in, mopping neck with handkerchief)
I might what?

JENNY
You might remember. *(Leaves it at that)*

RICHARD
(Thinks)
All right. *(Pause)* I might remember what?

JENNY
(Still looking for a cigarette)
When you throw them away.

RICHARD
(Considers that)
Um-hum. *(Pause)* May I go back out now? *Some*body's
got to get the damn lawn mowed, and I don't notice any
gardeners out there waiting for me to tell them what . . .

JENNY
(Finding every cigarette box empty)
I've told you two thousand times: well, I've told you *two*
things two thousand times: please keep cigarettes in the
house . . .

RICHARD
(Used to it, but airy)
You're running it.

JENNY
(Something of the strict schoolteacher creeping in)
When you finish a pack, do two things—I've told you . . .

RICHARD
—two thousand times—

JENNY
(Closes her eyes for a moment, goes on)
... first, when you finish a pack, look to see if it's the last one—the last pack ...

RICHARD
(Bored, impatient)
Yes, ma'am.

JENNY
(Undaunted)
And if it is, put it down to get some more, or tell *me* ...

RICHARD
(Ibid.)
O.K.; O.K.

JENNY
Whenever you *do* finish a pack, don't forget to take the coupons off. Please? The coupons? We save them?

RICHARD
Did I *forget?*

JENNY
You *always* forget. We smoke these awful things just to get the coupons ...

RICHARD
(Offhand)
O.K.

JENNY
(After a small pause)
Do you have any?

RICHARD

Coupons?

JENNY
(Not amused)

Cigarettes!

RICHARD
(Feels)

Um-hum. *(Suddenly aware)* Want one? *(Offers her the pack)*

JENNY
(Sees the pack)

Why, you dog! Those aren't . . . What are you—how dare you smoke *those* cigarettes, those don't have coupons, you . . . Do you mean I sit in here, ruining my lungs, piling up coupons, while you're sneaking around . . .

RICHARD
(Giggles at being caught)

Caught me, huh?

JENNY

You little . . . twerp!

RICHARD
(Lighting for her)

Big twerp. Good, aren't they?

JENNY
(Rue)

Yes. *(Pause)* How's the lawn?

RICHARD

Growing.

JENNY

Remember what I told you: watch out for the tulips.

RICHARD
(Exaggerated contrition)

Well, I gotta confess I got carried away, zooming along with the mower, *(Fast shiver sound)* br-br-br-br-br-br-br-br, mowed 'em down; by the time I got control of myself must have chopped up a good two dozen of 'em. *(Afterthought)* Sorry.

JENNY
(Nods knowingly)

Well, it wasn't funny that time you did. *(More-or-less to herself)* Honestly, a grown man running a lawnmower through a tulip bed.

RICHARD
(Jaunty and proud)

I rather liked it. Besides, what do you mean, "How's the lawn?" What do you care about the lawn? It could turn into one big dandelion patch for all you'd care so long as it didn't interfere with your hollyhocks and your tulips and your pink Williams, or whatever they are.

JENNY
(Superior, but friendly)

We all do what we're equipped for. Some of us are fit for keeping a lawn cut, and others . . . well, how green is my thumb.

RICHARD
(Looks at it all)

Looks good. Your scrambled eggs are a mess, but you sure can keep a garden.

JENNY
(Sweet-and-sour)
I'm just an outdoor type.

RICHARD
(Kisses her forehead)
Yes. You are. *(Collapses in an easy chair; groans with fatigue)* OOOOOHHHHhhhhhhhhhhhh, God!

JENNY

Hm?

RICHARD
(Sincere and sad)
I *wish* we could afford things.

JENNY
(Muted; ironic)
Keep smoking! Save those coupons!

RICHARD
Roger call? He get to school O.K.?

JENNY
Yes, he has three roommates this year, and they're going to let him have his bike.

RICHARD
(Very young again)
I wish they'd let me have a power mower.

JENNY
Well, you can't have one, so just . . . *(Leaves it unfinished)*

RICHARD

I am probably the only natural-born citizen east of the Rockies who does not have a power mower.

JENNY

Well, you cannot *have* one, so let it be.

RICHARD
(Points vaguely around, suggesting the neighborhood)
Alan has one; Clinton; *Mark!* Mark's got one he trades *in* every . . .

JENNY
(Surprisingly sharp)
No!

(Silence)

RICHARD
(To himself)
Forty-three years old and I haven't even got a power mower.

(Silence)

JENNY

Do you want something? Some tea, or a sandwich?

RICHARD
(Sharp)
Can we afford it?

JENNY
(Through her teeth)
Barely.

RICHARD
(Gets up, paces; offhand)

You, uh . . . you want to get a divorce? Get married again? Someone with money? Somebody with a power mower?

JENNY
(Weary, matter-of-fact)

Not this week; I'm too busy.

RICHARD
(Abstracted)

You let me know. *(Back to her)* How much?

JENNY

Hm?

RICHARD

How much do you spend? On, on seeds, and manure, and shears, and . . .

JENNY
(Gets up)

Oh, for God's . . .

RICHARD

. . . and, and bulbs, and stakes to hold the damn plants up, and . . .

JENNY
(Angry, but, still, rather bravura)

Plow it up! Plow the whole damn garden under! Put in gravel! And while you're at it, get rid of the grass!

RICHARD
(Shrugs)

Everybody has grass.

JENNY
(Furious)
EVERYBODY HAS A GARDEN! *(Still angry, but softer)* I am
willing; I am willing to scrimp, and eat what I don't
really want to half the time, and dress like something out
of a forties movie . . .

RICHARD
(Regretting the whole thing)
All right; all right . . .

JENNY
. . . and *not* have a maid, and only have my hair done
twice a month, and not say let's go away for the week-
end . . .

RICHARD
All right!

JENNY
. . . to pay and pay on this god-damned house . . .

RICHARD
(Soft, reasonable, but infuriating)
. . . everybody has a house . . .

JENNY
. . . *and* the bloody car . . .

RICHARD
. . . we need a car . . .

JENNY
. . . *and* Roger's school . . .

RICHARD
(Ire up a little)
When the public schools in this country . . .

JENNY
. . . *and* all the insurance . . .

RICHARD
We die, you know.

JENNY
. . . and everything else! Every money-eating thing!

RICHARD
Don't forget the government; *it's* hungry.

JENNY
I'll do it all, I'll . . . I'll smoke those awful cigarettes,
I'll . . . but I *will* not. I *will* not give up my garden.

RICHARD
(Gentle: placating)
I wouldn't *ask* you to.

JENNY
We live beyond our means, we have no right to be here,
we're so far in the hole you'll have to rob a bank or
something, we've . . .

RICHARD
I love your garden.

JENNY
(Quieting down some)
There are some things I will just not do: and first in
line is I will not give up my garden.

RICHARD

No; of course not.

JENNY

I *love* my garden.

RICHARD

Yes.

JENNY

The way the florist charges, if we had to buy *cut* flowers . . .

RICHARD

I *know; I know.*

JENNY

Now, if we had a greenhouse . . .

RICHARD

A greenhouse!

JENNY

Yes, well, a small one, just enough to raise some orchids
in . . .
        (*Sees* RICHARD *rise, move off shaking his head*)
. . . Where are you going?

RICHARD

I'm going out to kill myself.

JENNY

But why!?

RICHARD
(Losing control)
Do you know how much a greenhouse costs!?

JENNY
(Getting mad)
I'M TRYING TO SAVE MONEY!

RICHARD
(Dismissing her)
You're insane.

JENNY
Do you *know* how much cut flowers *cost*?

RICHARD
(Mimicking her)
Do you *know* how much a greenhouse *costs*?

JENNY
I am *trying* to save *money*.

RICHARD
(Tiny pause, then)
Then why don't you go to Paris and buy Christian Dior!?
That way you won't have to pay for your dresses.
(Silence)

JENNY
(Preoccupied)
Do you want some tea? Or a sandwich?
(RICHARD shakes his head; silence)
(A little sad, wistful, but reassuring)
We will have a greenhouse, someday. I'll make it nice;
you'll have a livingroom full of flowering plants; you'll
like it very much.

RICHARD
(Mildly ironic, sad)
Can I have a power mower first?

JENNY
(Nice)
You can have *everything*.

RICHARD
(Sighs)
That will be nice.

JENNY
(Wistful)
And so can I, and everything will be lovely.

RICHARD
(After a silence)
The thing I don't like about being poor . . .

JENNY
(Correcting by rote)
. . . about not having money . . .

RICHARD
The thing I don't like about being—about not having
money . . .

JENNY
(A little embarrassed, as if someone might overhear)
We're not *starving*.

RICHARD
No, we eat, but if we didn't belong to the, the *(Points
out the window)* club we'd eat a lot better.

JENNY
(Patient agreement)

Yes.

RICHARD

If we didn't try to live like our friends we might put
something away sometime.

JENNY
(Ibid.)

Um-hum.

RICHARD

Friends we didn't have, by the way, until we moved
here, took this place . . .

JENNY

But *friends*.

RICHARD

Oh, yeah, well, you find them. *(Tossed-off, but sincere)*
We don't live right.

JENNY
(Throws her head back, laughs)

Oh God!

RICHARD

We don't!

JENNY

Poor baby.

RICHARD
(As if in a debate)

You live in a forty-thousand-dollar house and you have

to smoke bad cigarettes to get the coupons so you can
afford a good vacuum so you can clean it; you belong
to the club so you can pay back dinner invitations from
people you wouldn't even know if you hadn't joined the
club in the first place, and you *joined* the club, *and*
learned how to play tennis, because you decided to move
into a neighborhood where everybody belonged to the
club.

JENNY
(Noncommittal)
Except the Jews and the tradespeople.

RICHARD
Hm? You're up to hock in your eyebrows . . . *(Realizes
what he has said, tries to fix it, retaining dignity) . . . up*
in hock to your . . . *in* hock up to your eyebrows, and
why!

JENNY
(Calm, nonplussed)
Because you want to live nicely.

RICHARD
I do?

JENNY
(Eyes closed briefly in martyrdom)
Because *we* do, because we want to live nicely; because
we want to live the way a lot of people manage . . .

RICHARD
Yes; people who can afford it!

JENNY
No! The way a lot of other people *cannot* afford it, and

still do. Do you think the mortgage department of the bank stays open just for us?

RICHARD

Look at Jack!

JENNY

Jack is rich! Look at everybody else.

RICHARD
(Pause; glum)

I don't feel I belong anywhere.

JENNY
(Slightly patronizing commiseration)

Awww; poor Richard.

RICHARD

It *does*, by the way.

JENNY
(Very straightforward, even a little suspicious)

What does what?

RICHARD

The bank; the mortgage department; stays open just for us.

JENNY
(Laughs a little)

You don't want a sandwich, or something?

RICHARD
(Preoccupied)

No.

JENNY
(Clear they've had this before)
I'm still able-bodied . . .

RICHARD
(Firm)
No.

JENNY
Lots of wives do it.

RICHARD
No.

JENNY
Just part-time, only from . . .

RICHARD
You may *not* get a job!

JENNY
It would make all the difference in . . .

RICHARD
(Out of patience, now)
No, now! *(Softer afterthought)* I'm not going to have a
wife of mine trying to work at some job, *and* running a
house, *and* looking after Roger when he's home from
school . . .

JENNY
Roger is fourteen, he doesn't need any looking after.

RICHARD
No! Besides, he's fifteen.

JENNY

And if I *took* a job, then we could afford a maid, and . . .

RICHARD

I said *no*.

JENNY
(Exasperated)

Well, it wouldn't be taking in laundry, for God's sake!

RICHARD
(Slightly nasty)

No? What would it be?

JENNY
(She, too)

Well, that may be all you think I'm good for . . .

RICHARD
(Voice rising)

I didn't *say* that.

JENNY

Well, you *inferred* it!

RICHARD

Implied; not inferred. And I did not.

JENNY

Yes you did, for God's sake.

RICHARD

I said nothing of the sort.

JENNY
(Snotty, exaggerated imitation)
No? Well, what would it *be?* What could you do? *(Anger)*
Is that all you think I'm good for?

RICHARD
(Trying patience now)
I didn't say that all you could do was take in laundry; I
merely meant that . . .

JENNY
(Starting to cry)
I'm sorry you think so badly of me.

RICHARD
(Eyes to heaven)
Oh, for Christ's . . .

JENNY
(Sniffling; the whole act which is not an act)
I'm sorry you think that's all I'm good for. I *try* to help
you; I try to run a decent house . . .

RICHARD
It's a *lovely* house . . .

JENNY
. . . and bring up your son so he won't be some . . . some
ruffian . . .

RICHARD
. . . *our* son . . .

JENNY
I try to *look* nice; I try to take care of myself, for *you*,
for your friends . . .

RICHARD

What, what is this everything *mine* all of a sudden! Most of the time it's yours; all yours!

JENNY
(Real tears again)

I try! I try!

RICHARD

Oh, Lord! *(Comes over, comforts her)* You do a *lovely* job; you run everything just . . . lovely; you look . . . you look good enough to eat. *(Snarls, tries to bite her neck)*

JENNY
(Martyr)

Don't, now.
                    (RICHARD *repeats snarl, bite*)
Just don't!
                          (RICHARD *moves away*)
Just . . . just go away.

RICHARD
(Pause; subdued)

I didn't mean to . . . say anything to upset you.

JENNY

No, but you *meant* it!

RICHARD
(Anger rising)

I did not *mean* it!

JENNY
(Angry, too)

Then why did you say it!!?

RICHARD
(Eyes narrowed)

What?

JENNY
(Cold)
If you didn't mean it, then why did you say it?

RICHARD
I didn't say what . . . you implied that I . . .

JENNY

Inferred!

RICHARD

SKIP IT!
(Silence)

JENNY
(Great soft-spoken dignity)
I was merely trying to suggest that I might be able to
help at the hospital one or two afternoons a week . . .

RICHARD
(Snorts)
And make enough to pay a maid out of that?

JENNY
(Trying to stay calm)
Or open a hat shop . . .

RICHARD
You're mad! You're absolutely mad!

JENNY
(Very sincere plea)

I just want to help?

(Silence)

RICHARD
(With her again; nicely)

I *know* you do. And you do as much as anyone; you do *more* than your share.

JENNY

No, no, I don't do *anything* to help you.

RICHARD
(Nuzzles)

You do *everything*.

JENNY

You think I'm worthless.

RICHARD
(To make light of it)

No, I imagine I could sell you for about . . . oh . . .

JENNY
(Won't go along)

You think I'm a drag; I'm not a helpmeet. Lots of women have part-time jobs, just to help out, it . . .

RICHARD
(Final)

No!

JENNY
(After a silence; sighs)

Money, money, money.

RICHARD

That's how it's always been. That's how it *is*.

JENNY
(Comforting)

You earn more than you used to.

RICHARD

Earn: yes. Taxes. Beware the steady man! Beware the slow
rise through the respectable ranks.
*(JACK appears in the french doors, enters, ob-
serves, lolls, speaks to the audience; becomes a
part of the action only when he speaks direct-
ly to one or another of the characters)*

JENNY

I know; Mother told me I should marry a real-estate
speculator.

RICHARD
(Going to the liquor cupboard)

Yes; well, well you should.

JENNY
(One more try)

So, if I had just a *little* job . . .

RICHARD
(Looking among bottles)

No!

JACK
(To the audience, while RICHARD *hunts among
the bottles)*

Are they arguing about money? Poor things; they always

do. They're very nice, though. Richard is decent, and
Jenny is . . . good. Damn it; wish she weren't.

JENNY
(Unaware of JACK*)*
What are you looking for?

RICHARD
(Ibid., not looking up from the bottles)
The vodka.

JENNY
There's some right there; right there in front of you.

RICHARD
Not *my* kind; not the Polish, only party stuff—American.

JENNY
("Get you")
Oh; well, sorry.

RICHARD
It's empty anyway.

JACK
(To the audience)
You see? That's it. The Polish vod is eight bucks a fifth.
That's what makes the difference: taste; and taste is
expensive. Poor children. *(A confidence)* I find Jenny *so
attractive*. Not that I'm going to jump her, or anything.
My letch is in the mind; *is; generally.*

RICHARD
(To JENNY*)*
Decent vodka is not a luxury.

JENNY

Nor is a greenhouse.

RICHARD

Yes it is.

JACK
(To the audience)

My uncle died and left *me* three-and-a-quarter mill.
Which is very nice. Which means *I* can have a greenhouse, *and* the Polish vodka, *plus* the thirty-year scotch,
plus . . . never worry—which is the nicest of all, don't
you think? *(In the action now)* Hello, children!

RICHARD

Hm?

JENNY
(Piqued and pleased, her reaction to JACK *is always a combination of maternal and coquettish)*

Oh, for God's sake, Jack!

RICHARD
(His reaction to JACK *is a combination of slight
mistrust, discomfort, and natural friendliness)*

Well, hello there, Jack.

JACK
(Sees they are a little embarrassed)

Ah, when I am wandering, footsore and loose, where do
I always come? *Here.* And why? Well, for a warm and
toasty welcome. How are you, children?

RICHARD

Poor.

JENNY

Fine!

JACK

Don't go together.

RICHARD

How've you been?

JACK
(Kisses JENNY *on the forehead)*
Stopped by the club to watch the heart attacks, looked
in on the poker game and dropped a couple of hundred.
(To JENNY*)* You . . . smell . . . lovely.

JENNY
(Pleased)

Thank you.

JACK

And . . . thought I'd come over the fence and see you
two.

RICHARD
(Nice, but an undertone)
I'll bet you'd like a drink.

JENNY
(To cover)

Ummm; me too!

JACK

Love one. Polish vod?

RICHARD
(A look at JENNY*)*
Fresh out.

JENNY
(To RICHARD*)*
Why don't you make us all a nice martini?

JACK
(Clucks; false disapproval)
Drink drink drink.

RICHARD
No vermouth either.

JACK
Such hospitality; I *tell* you.

RICHARD
I'll go get some.

JACK
Perfect! That way I get to be alone with your wife.

JENNY
Oh, Jack!

RICHARD
(To suggest, "If you are, I'll go get some")
You staying long?

JENNY
(Cheerful admonition)
Richard!

JACK

Well, what I thought I'd do is have one final drink with
the two of you. You see, I've settled a quarter of a million on each of you, and after I had my drink I thought
I'd go down in the cellar and kill myself.

JENNY

Awwwwww.

RICHARD
(A little grim)

You ought to do it somewhere else; we might have trouble getting the money if . . . *(Leaves it unfinished)*

JENNY
(Playing the game)

Yes . . . they might . . . *you* know . . . ask questions.

JACK
(To the audience)

He's right there, you know. Good mind. *(Back into action)* Oh. *(Pause)* Do you think? Yes; well, all right. I'll
just have the drink, then.

RICHARD
(Slight, uncertain pause)

O.K. *(Pause)* Well, I'll go get some.

JACK

Go, bucko; go.

JENNY
(Giggles)

Oh, honestly, Richard; I'll be all right.

JACK

You have a faithful wife, Richard; never fear. *(To the audience)* He has, too. She's rare; she's a good woman.

RICHARD
(Moving to exit, through hallway)
I know; it's the only kind I ever marry.

JACK
(Genuine surprise)
You been married before?

RICHARD
(Surprise)
No. I was just . . . *(At a loss for words)* . . . it was just a . . . something to say. *(To JENNY)* You, you want anything? At the store?

JENNY
(Shakes her head)
Unh-unh. Hurry back. Oh! Cigarettes!

RICHARD
(About to exit; a little bitter)
Which kind?

JENNY
(A giving-up sigh and smile)
The ones we like. Hurry, now.
                    (RICHARD exits)

JACK
(To the departed RICHARD)
By-ee! *(To JENNY, almost Groucho Marx)* Quick! He'll

be fifteen minutes even at a dog trot! Where's the guestroom?

JENNY
(Laughs)
Oh, come on, Jack! Besides, you aren't even a guest.

JACK
(Seemingly surprised)
No? What am I?

JENNY
A . . . uh . . . a fixture.

JACK
Something from the neighborhood? Bothersome Jack, here-
he-comes-again-probably-drunk-and-time-on-his-hands-so-
why-not-waste-everybody-else's-afternoon-while-he's-at-it?

JENNY
Mnnnnn.

JACK
(To the audience)
Am, too. Like that, I mean. Time, time. God, the ambi-
tion you have to have to overcome good fortune. I
haven't *got* it. *(Back to* JENNY*) Let* me paint your picture.

JENNY
(Cheerful, but it's clear they've had this before)
No.

JACK
Won't cost you a penny.

JENNY

No.

JACK
(To the audience)
I'm not a bad painter. Flattering portraits of the rich?
(Back to JENNY*)* What is it, then?

JENNY

I . . . just want to be different.

JACK
(Mild lechery)
Oh, you *are*, Jenny.

JENNY

Every, every house I go into, every time Richard and I
go out, there it is! Sybil, Grace Donovan, Junie, Mrs.
what's-her-name, Beachcomber, or something; *over* the
mantel, badly framed, the lady of the house; your por-
trait.

JACK
(Axiom)
Ladies *like* to be painted, *I* paint ladies, ladies hang pic-
tures.

JENNY
(Apologetic)
It isn't proper.

JACK
(Brief laugh)
Tell 'em in Newport; put me out of business. *(Digging)*
Besides, I bet I make more money in three good months
up there than Richard does in a whole . . .

JENNY

Oh, *money!*

JACK
(Waits a moment; quietly, smiling)
Yes? Money?

JENNY

I just don't . . . I don't want to look at myself, that's all.

JACK
(Very elegant)
If I were you . . . *I* would. *(Normal tone)* What's the matter, love?

JENNY

Oh . . . *(Very sincere, even plaintive, for a joke)* Would you do it, Jack? Go down in the cellar? I mean, leave Richard and me a quarter of a million each and then go kill yourself somewhere? I mean that nicely.

JACK

I'd do almost anything for you. *(Afterthought, but not flip)* Unless it got in the way of what I wanted to do for me. *(JENNY laughs ruefully)* What is it, puss?

JENNY
(Not going to talk about it)
Tired. Just . . . tired.

JACK

Want a shoulder to cry on?

JENNY

Nope; just a quarter of a million and an easy mind.

JACK
(Shakes his head knowingly)
Wouldn't help. Money's hungry, lonely, wants more of
itself. Stay poor; you're better off.

JENNY
(Snorts)
Crap!
(The doorbell rings; JENNY goes toward the hallway)

JACK
Really; you are.

JENNY
(Going)
You'd *know.*

JACK
I *watch. (JENNY has gone; JACK addresses the audience)*
I *have;* it *does;* money always wants more to keep it company. And a little money is a dangerous thing. Don't aim
for a million: that's the danger point. If I were to *die*
. . . *I* wouldn't leave them a quarter of a million each.
Bad. *I'd* leave 'em the whole damn three. As a matter of
fact, that isn't a bad idea at all. With three mill plus, they
wouldn't have to worry. I think I'll do it. Yes; consider
it done. *(Considers)* I am *healthy,* though. They might
not get it till it's way too late. Still . . . consider it done.

JENNY'S VOICE
(From the hallway)
No, of course not, don't be silly.
(JENNY appears, followed by MRS. TOOTHE)

MRS. TOOTHE
(Entering)
I *should* have phoned before just appearing at your door,
but I thought that on . . . Ah, this must be your husband.
How do you do, I'm Mrs. Toothe, and your wife has
been kind enough to . . .

JENNY
(A little laugh)
Oh, no, this isn't Richard—my husband, I mean . . .

MRS. TOOTHE
Ah. Well.

JENNY
(A little lame)
This is just . . . Jack.

MRS. TOOTHE
(Extends her hand to JACK)
No matter. How do you do, just the same.

JACK
(Takes hand, does curt little formal bow)
Mrs. Toothe.

JENNY
(Lame, and embarrassed by it)
Jack was just . . . passing by.

MRS. TOOTHE
(Noncommittal)
A friend of the family; of course.

JENNY
Yes.

JACK
(To MRS. TOOTHE*)*
Not at all: a secret admirer of lovely Jenny. I only come
round when Richard's out. We have a signal—panties on
the laundry line.

JENNY

Jack!

MRS. TOOTHE

How divine!

JENNY
(To MRS. TOOTHE; *embarrassed and furious at being)*
There isn't a word of truth to what he says. There isn't a
word of truth to *anything* he says, *ever.*

JACK
(Still to MRS. TOOTHE*)*
White panties if we've got one hour, yellow if we'll have
to hurry, pink for those special occasions . . .

JENNY

Jack! Please!

JACK
(Shakes his head, sadly)
I must confess it, madam, I am only what she says: a
friend of the family . . . dropping by. Damned attractive,
though. Wish it were true.

MRS. TOOTHE
(Pleased and sympathetic)
Ahhhh.

JENNY

Why is everybody standing? Please sit down, Mrs. . . .
uh . . . Toothe.

MRS. TOOTHE
(Sits)

Thank you.

JENNY

Jack, don't you think you should be . . . ?

JACK
(Makes it obvious he has gotten the signal)

By gum, I must be moving on! Different lines, more panties. There is no rest for the wicked in the suburbs. Mrs.
Toothe, it's been . . .

MRS. TOOTHE

A great pleasure. And don't get your signals mixed.
*(JENNY accompanies JACK to the doors to the
garden)*

JACK

Tell Richard I'll be back for that martini another day.
(Sotto voce) Who is she, your fairy godmother?

JENNY

Will you go?

JACK
(Pecks her on the forehead)

Bye. *(To the audience, a wave before quick exit)* Bye.
(JACK has gone; JENNY returns to MRS. TOOTHE)

JENNY

You mustn't believe a thing Jack says, Mrs. . . .

MRS. TOOTHE
(A hand up to silence her)
Oh, really. I can tell a lover from a friend.

JENNY
(Maybe even a little offended)
Oh? How?

MRS. TOOTHE
(Laughs)
Because in this country they're very seldom the same.

JENNY
You're English.

MRS. TOOTHE
Yes. Very.

(Small silence)

JENNY
Would you like some tea . . . or a drink?

MRS. TOOTHE
(Very efficient)
No thank you; this is business. Strictly business.

JENNY
(Pause)
Oh?

MRS. TOOTHE
I'm told you need a job?

JENNY
(Somewhat confused)
Who, who told you that?

MRS. TOOTHE
(Airy)
Oh, one of your friends. A woman.

JENNY
(Curious, still puzzled)
Oh? Who?

MRS. TOOTHE
No matter. Am I mistaken?

JENNY
(A little ill-at-ease)
Well, no . . . that is, I *was* thinking about getting a job . . .

MRS. TOOTHE
Yes, well, I thought so.

JENNY
Not a . . . a career, you understand, just something . . .

MRS. TOOTHE
. . . part *time,* something to bring a little extra money in.

JENNY
Well, yes; you know how it is: my son's away at school,
and I have the spare time. Besides, one can always use
money, can't one?

MRS. TOOTHE
(Looking about, noncommittally)
Yes; one can.

JENNY
These days, with taxes, and the private school . . .

MRS. TOOTHE

Oh, yes; yes; quite. What does your husband do?

JENNY
(Uncomfortable, as if being interviewed)
Well, he . . . he's a research chemist, and . . .

MRS. TOOTHE

. . . and that, as so many good things, pays less than it should.

JENNY
(Protecting RICHARD*)*
Well, he doesn't do *too* badly; I mean . . .

MRS. TOOTHE
(The laugh again)
Of course not! But, still; you would like a job.

JENNY
*(Looks to the hallway, guilty—*RICHARD *might come back)*
Well, yes; one . . . one likes to feel useful.

MRS. TOOTHE
(Looking into her handbag)
Yes; useful. *(She takes out a thick bundle of bills, shows them to* JENNY*)* Money. *(*JENNY *just looks at it, her mouth falling open a little)* For you. *(Makes to give it to her)*

JENNY

Yes, but . . . *(Laughs a little, astounded)*

MRS. TOOTHE
(Nods her head)
Yes, money. For *you*. A thousand dollars. Here, take it.

JENNY
(Withdrawing a little from it)
Well, no, I . . .

MRS. TOOTHE
Count it if you like. Here; a thousand dollars. *(Tries to force it on her)*

JENNY
(A little panicked)
No!

MRS. TOOTHE
Very well. *(As calm as can be; rises, goes with the money to the fireplace, throws it on the burning logs)*

JENNY
(Reflex, runs to the fireplace, almost puts her hands into the fire, makes a little yell; straightens up, holds on)
Oh—I think you'd better go, Mrs. Toothe.

MRS. TOOTHE
(Enigmatic smile)
Not yet. Let's begin again. *(She takes another bundle of money from her handbag, makes as if to throw it in the fire; JENNY holds out her hand; MRS. TOOTHE quietly hands her the money, resumes her seat; JENNY stays standing)*

JENNY
(Never taking her eyes off MRS. TOOTHE)
You're quite mad.

MRS. TOOTHE
No. Very rich.

JENNY
(Looks at the money, almost weighs it)
Look, you . . . you can't just . . . *give* me money like this.
I can't just . . .take money from you.

MRS. TOOTHE
(A little laugh)
You have. It's yours. Isn't there something you'd like to
buy? For yourself, for . . . what is his name? . . . Richard?

JENNY
People can't just give people money. I want to work.

MRS. TOOTHE
Good then.That's an advance of salary. You can work
for me.

JENNY
But I haven't *said* I'd take a job at *all*. Richard is *very*
much against it, and . . .

MRS. TOOTHE
(Daring her to refuse)
I was told you needed money.

JENNY
Yes, but Richard wouldn't approve of anything like this,
and . . .

MRS. TOOTHE

Like what? *(Indicates the money)* Wouldn't he approve
of *that?*

JENNY
(Looks at the money in her hands)

I'm sorry; I didn't mean to be rude, but it's all so vague,
isn't it? And . . . and so unexpected.

MRS. TOOTHE
(Shrugs)

It's a job.

JENNY
(Nervous laughter in her voice)

Well, you'll have to tell me what it *is.* I mean, money
isn't everything.

MRS. TOOTHE

No? What isn't money? Here we are; this house is money, that garden, that lovely garden, those clothes you're
wearing, it's all *money,* isn't it?

JENNY

The job?

MRS. TOOTHE

What are your husband's hours?

JENNY

He leaves at eight and gets home from town at seven-
thirty, but . . .

MRS. TOOTHE

Very good. *You'll* come in town, four afternoons a week,

from one to five, say. You'll come to my address—lovely
street: psychiatrist's office, doctors . . .

JENNY

Is this a . . . uh . . . a receptionist's job?

MRS. TOOTHE

Receptionist?

JENNY

Making, making appointments, and so on?

MRS. TOOTHE

I make appointments. For *you.*

JENNY
(Tiny pause)

For me? Who with?

MRS. TOOTHE

Clients.

JENNY
(Innocent)

What *for?*

MRS. TOOTHE

For a hundred dollars.

JENNY

No, I mean . . . A hundred dollars?

MRS. TOOTHE

More, sometimes—if they're generous.

JENNY

But these clients . . . who are they?

MRS. TOOTHE

Some businessmen, some visitors. All gentlemen; all
rich.

JENNY
(The knowledge is there but not admitted yet)
What . . . exactly . . . what exactly would I do . . . for
this money?
> *(MRS. TOOTHE laughs lightly; JENNY's jaw
> drops with the admission; pause)*
> *(JENNY picks up the bundle of money, holds it
> out to MRS. TOOTHE; even, hard)*
Get out of my house.
> *(MRS. TOOTHE does nothing; JENNY drops the
> money on the table)*
I'll call the police.

MRS. TOOTHE
(As calm as anything; a little superior)
Whatever for?

JENNY
(Quivering)
You know what for!

MRS. TOOTHE
(Smiles)
I've said nothing.

JENNY
You know what you've suggested!

MRS. TOOTHE
(Shrugs)

That you make money.

JENNY

THAT WAY!

MRS. TOOTHE

You have a friend who does.

JENNY

Who!

MRS. TOOTHE

Oh, no; we're very discreet.

JENNY
(Through her teeth)

I don't believe you, not a word! People around here wouldn't do that sort of *thing;* you don't realize; you don't know what we're like.

MRS. TOOTHE
(Unconcerned)

Have it your way.

JENNY

One of the tradespeople, maybe; you're thinking of someone like that.

MRS. TOOTHE

I'm thinking of a friend of your; a very nice woman with a lovely house, who keeps it nicely—much more nicely than this, by the way—a woman who has no more worries about money, who is very happy. So could you be.

JENNY

You're a filthy woman! IT'S DISGUSTING!!

MRS. TOOTHE
(Very calm)
Nothing is disgusting, unless one is disgusted.

JENNY

YOU'RE EVIL!!

MRS. TOOTHE

Yes, yes ...

JENNY

I'LL TELL THE POLICE!

MRS. TOOTHE
(Stands up, stretches a little)
Good. Then perhaps they'll arrest me.

JENNY

I hope they put you in prison!

MRS. TOOTHE

Yes, well, they probably will, and then I shall admit
everything.

JENNY

Everything?

MRS. TOOTHE

Yes, how you approached me, and we discussed it, but
the terms didn't suit you. The *money* wasn't enough.

JENNY

THAT'S NOT TRUE!

MRS. TOOTHE

Perhaps not. I think it would be believed, though. By
enough people.

JENNY

GET OUT OF HERE!

MRS. TOOTHE
(Takes a calling card from her handbag)
Here is my card; address; telephone; let me know what
you decide.

JENNY
(Change of tone; almost tearful)
Please? Please go?

MRS. TOOTHE

No police then; good. *(Sees* JENNY *will not take the card,
puts it down next to the bundle of money on the table)*
Don't telephone me before ten, though, please. I *do*
like my sleep.

JENNY

Please? Go?

MRS. TOOTHE
(Smiles)
I'll see myself out. It's been very nice to meet you. *(Looks
one final time at the garden)* What a lovely garden. Do
you have a greenhouse?
     (Smiles, exits, leaving JENNY *standing in the
     center of the room)*
     *(*JENNY *looks after* MRS. TOOTHE *for a long mo-
     ment, not moving. Then she looks down at the
     table whereon sit the bundle of money and* MRS.
     TOOTHE's *card. She picks up the card, reads*

*it, moving her lips, then, with a grimace, rips
the card in half and, as if she were carrying
feces, takes it over to a wastebasket and drops
it in. She comes back to the table, stares at the
money, picks it up, looks at it with detached fascination; doesn't know quite what to do with it;
finally, rather firmly, puts it in desk drawer,
locks drawer, keeps key, starts toward french
doors, looks back at locked drawer, goes, stands
at french windows looking out)*

RICHARD'S VOICE
(From the hallway)

Hell-oo-oo. *(He enters, with a paper bag of liquor)* Oh,
there you are. And who the hell was *that* tripping down
our path, that bit of old England? "How do you do?"
she . . . Where the hell *is* he—Jack?

JENNY
(Sort of vacant)

Oh. Hi.

RICHARD
(Puts liquor down, starts taking bottles out of bag)

Well, who *was* she—your fairy godmother?

JENNY
(Some alarm)

My what?

RICHARD

The woman; the lady. Who was she?

JENNY
(Still preoccupied)

Oh. Mrs. Toothe.

RICHARD

Mrs. what?

JENNY

Toothe; Toothe.

RICHARD

You're kidding. Where's Jack?

JENNY

It's a perfectly proper English name. *(Pause)* I guess.
Jack? He *went.*

RICHARD

Figures. Send me out to buy up the liquor store and off
he goes.

JENNY

It was *your* idea to go.

RICHARD
(A little cross)

Who *was* she?

JENNY

Mrs. Toothe? *(Tosses it off)* Oh . . . committee; wants
me for the hospital.

RICHARD

Free? Or pay?

JENNY
(Pause; casual)

Pay.

RICHARD

No!

JENNY
(Pause; softly)

All right.

RICHARD
(Looks at the liquor)

Well, with all your rich guests gone, there's just us for drinks. What do you want . . . a martini?

JENNY
(Very sincere)

Yes, I think that would be *nice.*

RICHARD

O.K. *(Starts to make one; the ice is already there)* You know what Tom Palmer said the other day?

JENNY
(Preoccupied, *and not exactly unpleasant, but not pleasant either)*

No, I don't; I didn't see Tom Palmer the other day. What did Tom Palmer say?

RICHARD
(Looks up at JENNY *for a moment, quizzically, then back to his work)*

He said Jack was at the club, at the bar . . . soused as usual . . .

JENNY

Jack isn't always drunk.

RICHARD
(A little annoyance)
He's always drinking.

JENNY
(Dogmatic)
That does *not* make him *drunk*.

RICHARD
I am merely repeating what Tom Palmer said.

JENNY
Tom Palmer's an old woman.

RICHARD
(Quite annoyed)
I do *not* want to argue!

JENNY
All right! *(Contrite)* I'm sorry, darling. *(Pause)* You're a good, decent man and I love you.

RICHARD
(Grudging)
Well, you're a good, decent woman, and I love you, too. As a matter of fact, I shall give you a house-special martini to show you how *much* I love you.

JENNY
Oh, I would like that.
(She comes for her drink, takes it from him; they put arms around each other, move toward the sofa; he kisses her on top of her head)

RICHARD
I think you smell even nicer than Jack does.

JENNY
(Purring)
When have you smelled Jack?

RICHARD
Than *Jack* thinks you smell.

JENNY
Oh.
                    (RICHARD *tries to nip her neck*)
Ow! Now stop that; I'll spill my martini.
                    (They sit on the sofa, relax)

RICHARD
(A little bitter)
You want to know something really funny?

JENNY
I don't *think* so. What?

RICHARD
I was in the liquor store . . .

JENNY
That's a riot.

RICHARD
Hush. I was in the liquor store, and Grady, who owns it,
do you know what he told me?

JENNY
No; what?

RICHARD
He's getting a second car? Not trading one in; getting a
second car.

JENNY

So?

RICHARD

Guy who owns a crummy little liquor store can have two
cars? And we have to get by with . . .

JENNY

Did you bring the cigarettes back with you?

RICHARD

Hm? *(Gets them out)* Oh; yes; here.

JENNY
(Takes one; so does he; he lights them both)
I wonder which kills more people: liquor or cars?

RICHARD

Well, when you put them together it's pretty good. What's
for dinner?
(Pause)

JENNY

Let's go *out* for dinner.

RICHARD

Where?

JENNY
(Expansive)
Let's . . . let's go to Le Cavalier.

RICHARD
(Snorts)
You must be out of your mind.

JENNY

No! Let's!

RICHARD

It'll cost twenty-five dollars each. After a drink, the wine, it'll cost twenty-five each!
> (Pause)

JENNY
> (Cautiously)

I've got some money.

RICHARD
> (Half hearing)

Hm?

JENNY

I said, *I've* got some money.

RICHARD
> (Vaguely interested)

How?

JENNY
> (Very offhand)

Oh, I've . . . put a little aside out of household. I keep a little bit each week.

RICHARD
> (Mildly)

Well, I'll be damned.

JENNY

Come on; let's go out; it'll do us good. Let's go to Le Cavalier. Let's live it up.

RICHARD

Let's pretend we can afford it?

JENNY

Sure! Come on; it'll do us both good.

RICHARD

You ingenious thing. How much have you got?

JENNY

Oh . . . enough. Come on now.

RICHARD

You clever girl. *(Rises)* I'd better wash up. Really? You
have enough?

JENNY
(Rises)
Yes. Better put things away in the garden before you get
cleaned up.

RICHARD

Right. *(Moves to the french doors)* You very clever girl.
(Goes outside)

> *(JENNY sees he is out of sight; goes slowly to
> the desk, unlocks the drawer, takes out the bun-
> dle of money, strips off several bills, puts them
> on the table, hesitates a moment, as to reconsid-
> er, then puts the rest of the money back in the
> drawer, locks it again, keeps the key. Stands for
> a moment; looks at the wastebasket, lifts it onto
> the table, takes the two halves of* MRS. TOOTHE's
> *card out, fits them together, looks at the card.*
> RICHARD *pokes his head inside;* JENNY *doesn't
> flinch or try to hide the card, knowing that*

RICHARD *either can't see it or won't ask what it is)*

RICHARD

Jenny?

JENNY

Hm?

RICHARD
(Sort of wistful)
Darling? How much does a greenhouse cost? You know
. . . a little one?

JENNY

Why?

RICHARD

I just wondered.

JENNY
(Looks up)
Quite a bit.

RICHARD

I just wondered. *(Returns outside)*

JENNY
(Looks at the card again, shakes her head; some rue)
Quite a bit.

CURTAIN

SCENE TWO

(Six months later; scene the same; early afternoon;
RICHARD *at the desk, paying bills; shakes his head occa-*
sionally, despair. Sound of front door opening, closing.
JENNY *comes in, with bundles)*

JENNY
(Cheerful)
Hello.

RICHARD
(Glum)
Hello.

JENNY
On Saturday you're supposed to rest; why aren't you out
working in the garden?
                    (RICHARD laughs glumly)
Or, or just . . . lying around?

RICHARD
(Wan smile)
Paying bills.

JENNY
Oh. *(Puts bundles down)* It figures, doesn't it: I go to
the store and I forget half of what I want.

59

RICHARD

Didn't you make a list?

JENNY

Of course; I *got* everything on the list; I just didn't remember to put everything *on* the list.

RICHARD

Like what?

JENNY

Like what? Like . . . like root beer, and extra milk, and
stuff for cookies, and . . .

RICHARD

What for?

JENNY

We have a son. Right?

RICHARD
(Preoccupied)

Um-huh.

JENNY
(Pause)

He's coming *home* today!

RICHARD
(Puzzlement, pleasure)

Roger? Today? Coming home?

JENNY
(As if he were addled)

Yes. Vacation.

RICHARD

Well, I'll be damned.

JENNY

Mmmmmmm. And cornflakes and stuff, I suppose.

RICHARD

No camp this year.

JENNY

Hm?

RICHARD

No camp this year. For Roger. No camp. Can't afford it.

JENNY
(Noncommittal; her mind on something else)
Oh. Really?

RICHARD

Really.

JENNY
(Making her list)
Well, afford or not, I thought it'd be nice if he was around
here this summer. Get to know him.

RICHARD
(Adamantly grousing)
Well, nice or not . . . necessary.

JENNY

Help *you*, help *me* . . .

RICHARD

While you're at it, get some more envelopes.

JENNY

There *are* some.

RICHARD

No, just that . . . that paper thing goes around them.

JENNY
(Notes it down)
All right. He can help you in the garden.

RICHARD

Mmmm. Or maybe we can get him a magazine route.

JENNY
(Mild disgust and indignation)
Really!

RICHARD

Well, you're so keen for everybody to be working around here . . .

JENNY

He's just a child!

RICHARD

He's probably going steady already—got some local girl up at school—probably skips out at night, shacked up . . .

JENNY
(Protesting, embarrassed)
Richard!

RICHARD

Kids grow up early nowadays.

JENNY

Roger is fourteen years old!

RICHARD

Well, if everything's functioning properly, there's no reason why he can't be getting laid, is there? Besides, he's fifteen.

JENNY

That's enough now.

RICHARD

Well, it's better that than lots of other things.

JENNY

ALL RIGHT!

(Silence)

RICHARD
(Shakes his head, finally, a little sadly, smiles)
I knew a girl once, when you and I were dating—not so as to say set the alarm for seven, or anything like that, but . . .

JENNY
(A little stony)
Don't regale me.

RICHARD

No; really. And I wasn't in on the good times, 'cause I was counting on *you* . . .
(JENNY snorts)
. . . and you met her, I think, but I won't tell you who she was, cause she still *is* . . . but she had the reputation as a proper put-out . . .

JENNY
(Some bored annoyance)

Please, Richard.

RICHARD

No. *More* than proper: something of a dedicatee, guest
bedrooms at parties, drawing blood, literally . . .

JENNY

Let the poor woman *alone*.

RICHARD
(Slight edge)

I'm not *touching* her. *(Silence)* I was planning, though, to
compare her to *you*.

JENNY
(Sarcastic)

Really.

RICHARD

To your ad*van*tage.

JENNY
(Dripping irony)

Oooohhhh.

RICHARD

Socially—by which I mean out of bed, which is a euphe-
mism for trash heaps and coal bins—you'd think she was
the Queen Mother. Staid? She practically used the royal
We. So proper; you'd never know.

JENNY
(Not nice)

And what does that have to do with me?

RICHARD

Oh. It came up when I said Roger was probably going steady.

JENNY

Getting laid is what you said.

RICHARD

Same difference.

JENNY

Tell *that* to the sociologists.

RICHARD

They know. And I said Roger was probably going steady and you came on all funny and red and ...

JENNY

I didn't see any need for you to shout the house down, and ...

RICHARD
(Angry)

Who's going to hear? The footmen?

JENNY

Don't you yell at me!

RICHARD
(Pause; shake of head; laugh-whimper)

All I wanted to do was say you're such a funny, silly, wonderful little ...

JENNY

Nuts.

RICHARD

You are! You're a good wife and you're nice in bed, but you're funny and . . . prim.

JENNY

Prim!?

RICHARD

Yes! Prim!

JENNY

I'm *sorry*.

RICHARD

And then I thought about, uh, what's-her-name, who came on like the Queen Mother, and how she was ridiculous and you were just a little silly about it, and . . . *(Mumbles)* aw, for Christ's sake, forget it. *(Pause)* I was just trying to pay you a *comp*liment! I was *try*ing to be *nice!*

JENNY
(Thinks about it, dismisses his reasoning)
I don't see why you brought her up in the *first* place.

RICHARD
(Frustrated anger)

NEITHER DO I!

(Silence)

JENNY

I suppose I could learn a few dirty jokes, or start telling people about a couple of your peculiarities when it comes to . . .

RICHARD

Forget it!

(Silence)

JENNY
(Trying to hold back a smile)

Who was she?
(RICHARD pouts, shakes his head)
Come on; who was she?

RICHARD

No, no.

JENNY
(Tickles him a little)

Oh, come on!

RICHARD
(Happier)

No; now, stop it.
(She tickles more, he grabs her, they wrestle,
giggling, a little on the sofa, playing, ending in
a kiss, then another, which prolongs, is far more
serious)

JENNY

Unh-unh; not now.

RICHARD

Ooooohhhh . . .

JENNY

No; Roger'll come in, and . . .

RICHARD

Well, he'll be able to tell his friends we're still alive.

JENNY

Now, come *on. No.*

RICHARD
(Leans back; sighs)

All right.

JENNY
(Pause)

Who was she?

RICHARD
(Shakes his head)

Unh-unh. I promised.

JENNY
(Eyes narrowing)

Who?

RICHARD

Myself. Self-discipline.

JENNY
(Disentangling)

Oh, honestly!

RICHARD

Well, a little doesn't hurt.

JENNY
*(Looking at herself in the mirror, appraisingly,
approvingly)*

Did you see the paper today?

RICHARD
(Preoccupied)

Mmmmm.

JENNY

They had an ad.

RICHARD
(Back to the desk)

What are they doing, giving away money? I can sure
use some, if they . . .

JENNY
(Still appraising)

No, for a greenhouse, all-aluminum frame, curved
glass . . .

RICHARD
(Slams a sheet of paper down)

For Christ's sake, Jenny!
(Pause, as she looks at him, a little haughtily)
I just finished telling you Roger isn't going to camp this
year because we can't afford it, and . . .

JENNY
(Slight airy contempt)

Oh, money-money-money.

RICHARD

Yes. Money. *(Shows bills)* Oil. The car. Con Ed—the
bastards. An estimate on the attic—the leak.
(Doorbell rings)

JENNY

Doorbell.

RICHARD
(Back to work)
Yes. Why don't you get it?

JENNY
(Tiny pause)
Why don't you?

RICHARD
Hm?

JENNY
Why don't *you* get it?

RICHARD
(Slight whine)
Because I'm working, darling; can't you see I'm . . .

JENNY
What if it's for you?

RICHARD
(Slight bewilderment)
Then you can tell me who it *is*. Or *what*.

JENNY
(Pause, hesitation)
Oh. Yes, that's true.
(Doorbell again)

RICHARD
(Throws pen down, gets up, goes out)
Oh, for God's sake!
(Maybe, offstage, we hear RICHARD *saying
"Yes?" and then "Oh, O.K." While he is off-*

stage JENNY *moves about the room a little,
practicing unconcern.* RICHARD *re-enters, with a
small package: brown paper, wrapped with
twine, lots of stamps, special delivery, etc.)*

JENNY

Who was it?

RICHARD
*(Looking at package, with some curiosity and
distaste)*
Package.

JENNY

Oh, for me?

RICHARD

No. For me. *(Shakes it, looks at it again)*

JENNY
(Pause)
Well. *(Pause)* Open it.

RICHARD
*(Putting it down on the table, stares at it, hands
on hips)*
Wonder what it is.

JENNY
(Little laugh)
Well, open it and see.

RICHARD
(Picks it up again, looks it over)
Special delivery, doesn't say where from.

JENNY

Well, open it, for heaven sakes.

RICHARD
(Tries to break twine, can't)

It's . . . tied up so . . .
(Takes a pocket knife, saws through twine, be-
gins to unwrap. JENNY keeps a distance. RICH-
ARD reveals contents. Slow awe in movements)

JENNY
(Trying for unconcern)

What, what is it?

RICHARD
(Wonder)

Jenny! Look!

JENNY

Hm?

RICHARD

Jenny! It's money!

JENNY

It's what?

RICHARD

IT'S MONEY!!

JENNY
(Feigning disbelief and childish pleasure)

Money. It's money?

RICHARD
(Subdued; awe)
Jenny; it's money. It's a great deal of money.

JENNY
(Taking a step closer)
Well, for . . . for heaven sake.

RICHARD
Jenny, it's ten-dollar bills, wrapped in packages of five hundred dollars each.

JENNY
(Beautiful bewilderment)
Well . . . how *much?* How much *is* there?

RICHARD
(Starts counting, aloud then silently)
One, two, three, four, five, six, seven, eight, nine . . .

JENNY
(During his counting. Pauses between)
How . . . how incredible. I've . . . How absolutely incredible.

RICHARD
And wait . . . Here are hundred-dollar bills. One, two, three, four . . . *(Slight confusion)* Forty-nine hundred dollars.

JENNY
(Some confusion)
Forty-nine?

RICHARD

Jenny, there's almost five thousand dollars here. Four
thousand, nine hundred dollars. Jenny! Four thousand,
nine hundred dollars!

JENNY

Well, that's incredible! Not five thousand?

RICHARD
(Sudden suspicion something's wrong)
I don't get it.

JENNY

Aren't you ... aren't you pleased?

RICHARD
(Wry comment on her word)
Pleased!? I don't know whether I'm pleased or not.

JENNY
(Still not near the money)
Is it real? Is it real money?

RICHARD
(Looks at a bill)
Yes; of course it's real: real used hundred-dollar bills.

JENNY
(A kind of satisfaction)
My God.

RICHARD

But .. but *why?* I mean, there's no *sense* to it.

JENNY
(A protective step forward)
Yes, but it *is money*.

RICHARD
(Looks at it glumly)
It's money, all right. Too bad we can't keep it.

JENNY
What do you mean?

RICHARD
(No great enthusiasm)
I mean we can't keep it. I'll take it to the police.

JENNY
No!

RICHARD
I *have* to, Jenny. There's something wrong here.

JENNY
What!

RICHARD
(At a loss for words)
Well ... I mean ...

JENNY
It's addressed to you, isn't it? It came special delivery; it's not as though you *found* it, for God's sake.

RICHARD
Yes, I know, but ...

JENNY
(As offhand as likely)
Well, it seems to me someone wants you to have it. I . . .
I can't think of any other reason for someone to send it
to you.

RICHARD
Wants me to *have* it. Yes, but who?

JENNY
I . . . I don't know. *(Shrugs)* Someone.

RICHARD
Look, it could be something awful like . . .

JENNY
Like what?

RICHARD
Like, like the Mafia, or something, or bank robbers, or
. . . sent it here for sakekeeping, and . . .

JENNY
(Laughs gaily)
Don't be ridiculous.

RICHARD
(Thinks about it; subdued)
You think someone *sent* it to me?

JENNY
(The most obvious thing in the world)
Of *course.*

RICHARD
Yes, but *who?*

JENNY

Well ... maybe ... somebody you did something for.

RICHARD

Those sort of things don't happen ... not to *me*.

JENNY

Well, *this* has happened.

RICHARD
(Holds the money out to her; quite childlike)
Don't you want to ... touch it, or anything?

JENNY

Oh. Yes; of course. *(Goes to him, touches the money, smiles faintly)* I wonder who sent it to you.

RICHARD

I ... I don't *know*. There's a man I sit next to on the train a lot. *He* seems very interested in me; older fellow, banker type. Keeps asking me about my work, how I manage. Maybe, maybe he's a millionaire, and maybe he's sort of crazy.

JENNY
(Unlit cigarette out)
Match.

RICHARD

Hm? Oh, yeah. *(Is about to hand her the matchbook, thinks better of it, lights her cigarette)* It could come from somebody like him.

JENNY
(Slightest doubt)
Well, yes, it could.

RICHARD
(Puzzled, a little deflated)
And then again it couldn't. I mean, probably didn't.

JENNY
(Comforting)
Yes. But someone.

RICHARD
Yes. *(Considers, gives her a bill)* Here. For you.

JENNY
(Tiniest pause)
Thank you. You're . . . you're not going to turn it over to the police, then.

RICHARD
(Pause, slight guilt, but bravura)
No, I don't think so. *(Pause)* I guess someone wants me to have it. Someone *must*. It'd be silly not to keep it. *(Pause)* Don't you think so?

JENNY
(Nice smile)
Yes. I think so.

RICHARD
I mean, it would be stupid to just . . . throw it away.

JENNY
Yes; it would be. *(Cheerful)* Let's have a drink: to celebrate?

RICHARD
(The sky has cleared)
Yes! Let's.

JENNY
(Moves toward hall)
I'll get the ice.

RICHARD
(Moves toward the liquor cabinet)
Good— And I'll make us a four-thousand-nine-hundred-dollar martini.

JENNY
Super! *(Exiting)* Call it five thousand even; sounds so much nicer.
  *(JACK enters through the french doors after
  JENNY exits and RICHARD follows)*

JACK
(Sauntering into the room; addresses the audience)
The months turn; people live and die, but I just . . . wander around. I tell you, there are days when I admit to myself that I don't think I'm alive—never have been. *Un voyeur de la vie . . .* that's me. Look on; look in. *(Propounds a great truth, with nothing other than objectivity)* I've never felt really alive. It can't be only the isolation, the isolation of money, do you know? Naw, can't be that. I know lots of people with much more than I've got, and they've been alive . . . killed themselves and everything! Oh, by the way, I did what I said I was going to. *(Nods)* I made my will—remade it, to be technical—and left the whole kaboodle to Jenny and Richard here. Three million plus. I'd better not tell them, though. It's hard enough to like me as it is. I mean, I'm likable and all, but . . . *(Spies the money on the table)* My goodness. *(Speaks loudly, is now in the action)* My goodness! Look at all that money!

RICHARD
(Enters from kitchen)
DON'T TOUCH THAT!

JACK
(Feigned affront)
I'm sorry!

RICHARD
(Still stern, advances toward the money)
Just don't touch it.

JACK
Well. Shall I go back out and knock?

RICHARD
(Sighs, laughs a little)
I'm sorry, Jack.
          (JENNY *re-enters, with the ice bucket*)

JENNY
Here we go, five thousand dollars' worth of ice, an . . .
oh. Jack.

JACK
(Sees they are both ill at ease. To audience)
My goodness.

JENNY
(Tiny pause; show of great bonhomie)
Hi!

RICHARD
Join us.

JACK
(Smiles, waiting to have things explained)

O.K.

RICHARD
(To JENNY)

Jack, uh, noticed the money here, and . . .

JACK
(Very pleasantly)

. . . and practically got my head snapped off.

JENNY

Oh. Well; there it is; money.

JACK
(Looks at it)

Did you steal it, or make it in the basement on your
own little press?

RICHARD

Neither, we . . .

JENNY

It arrived; it just . . . arrived.

RICHARD
(To explain further)

In the mail.

JENNY

Yes.

RICHARD
(Ibid.)

Special delivery.

JENNY

Yes.

JACK
  (Tiny pause; clearly, there must be more explanation)
Well, that's very nice.

JENNY

Someone sent it to Richard.

JACK

Oh?

RICHARD

Yes.

JACK

Who?

JENNY

Well, we don't know, someone, we figure, who . . . well, appreciates him. Admires him, maybe.

JACK

You mean you have no idea where it came from.

JENNY

No.

RICHARD

None.

JENNY

Absolutely none.

JACK

Is there a lot? Can I touch it?

RICHARD
(Involuntary gesture to protect money, with-draws it)
Sure.

JACK
(Touches it with one finger, looks at finger)
Perfectly dry.

JENNY

Of course; it's real.

RICHARD
(Sudden, none-too-happy thought)
Jack . . . *you* didn't do this, did you?

JACK

Do what?

RICHARD

You didn't. *You* didn't send us this money, did you?

JACK
(Tiny pause, then a laugh)
Christ, no!

RICHARD

You're sure, because if you did . . .

JACK

I'm sure; I'm absolutely sure. *(To audience)* I didn't,

by the way; I didn't send it to them. *(Back to them)*
How much is there?

JENNY

Nearly ...

RICHARD

Five thousand.

JACK

Well, that should prove it to you. I never deal in small
amounts.

RICHARD
(Defensive)

It might seem a small amount to *you,* but, to *some* people ...

JENNY
(To change the subject)

Why don't we all have a nice martini?

JACK

Splendid!
        (RICHARD *sets about to make them.* JENNY
        straightens up the room)
I didn't mean to ridicule your ... your windfall.

JENNY

Oh, now ...

JACK

It's just splendid. *(To the audience)* And damned pecu-
liar too, if you ask me. *(Back into the action)* Well, I
do hope you're going to give a party.

(RICHARD *and* JENNY *look at one another,
enthusiasm first*)

JENNY

Why, yes; we could!

RICHARD
(Hesitating)
Well, I don't think we ought to an*nounce* that . . .

JACK

No, just a party for the hell of it. Live it up a little!
Get some caviar! Serve champagne! Hire a butler! Give a
garden party!

JENNY
(Entranced)

A garden party!

RICHARD
(Giving over to it)
Sure! Why not!

JACK

Sure! Why not! *(To the audience; shrugs)* Why not?

JENNY

What a super idea. When?

JACK

Now.

JENNY

Well, no . . . Next week, and . . .

RICHARD
(Wistful; a little sad)
You know . . . people make plans, and . . .

JACK
No; *now.* This very minute: white heat. Get on the
phone. Give a blow-out; just for the hell of it! *(Gentler)*
Do something wild, and out-of-the-ordinary, and . . . the
sort of thing you've always *wished* you could do.

JENNY
Yes! Let's! I'll call . . . who shall I call?

RICHARD
Well . . . Chuck and Beryl . . .

JENNY
(On her fingers; enthusiasm)
Yes, Chuck and Beryl, and Cynthia and Perry, too, of
course . . .

RICHARD
. . . yes . . .

JENNY
. . . and . . . and Gilbert and Louise. Who else?

RICHARD
(Little laugh)
Hey, come on now. Let's not spend it all in one place.

JENNY
Is that enough? Six? Oh, and Jack; *you'll* come, Jack.

JACK

No, my darling; I've got a serious game of backgammon at the club.

JENNY

. . . oooohhhh . . .

JACK

No; *very* serious. High stakes. Wouldn't miss it for the world.

JENNY
(A colt)

I'll go call. O.K.?

RICHARD
(Amused)

O.K.

JENNY
(To RICHARD*)*

You figure out what we need, how much liquor and all . . .

RICHARD

Not champagne?

JENNY

Yes! Of course! But some people don't like it. I'll go call. *(Starts out of the livingroom)*

RICHARD

What time?

JENNY

Oh . . . six, six-thirty. What is it now?

RICHARD

Four.

JENNY
(Momentary pause)
Oh. *(Resolve)* Well, better hurry. *(As she goes)* Bye,
Jack!

JACK

Bye! *(To* RICHARD*)* Does that mean I'm supposed to be
gone by the time she gets back from phoning?

RICHARD
(Merely laughs; hands JACK *his martini)*
Here.

JACK
(Takes it)
Ice-cold, juniper-berried heaven. Thank you.
(We will hear JENNY *faintly from the other
room, talking to people on the phone. We will
hear her enthusiasm)*

RICHARD

She's so excited. Cheers.

JACK

Double. Well, why shouldn't she be? Quite marvelous
getting money this way.

RICHARD

Yes.

JACK

No tax, I mean. Tax-free?

RICHARD

Hm?

JACK

Well, you won't de*clare* it, of course . . . and that way there's no tax.

RICHARD
(He'd never thought of that)
You're right! Free and clear. God!

JACK

And maybe there'll be *more*.

RICHARD
(A little puzzled)

More? Why?

JACK

Well, good God . . . if someone's sending you money like this, why should they stop with one bundle? Maybe you'll get it every week.

RICHARD
(Almost blushes)

Oh, come on.

JACK

No; I mean it!

RICHARD
(Worried frown)
Jack, you won't . . . you won't tell anybody about this, will you?

JACK
(Jaunty)

My dearest Richard . . . it'll fly out of mind in thirty
seconds. No, of *course* I won't say anything. I don't
want to screw it up for you.

RICHARD

I mean not even casually, or reference to it, you know,
at the club, or . . .

JACK

. . . or when I've had a drink or two? No, Richard; I
won't. I promise.

RICHARD

Thanks.

JACK
(Lolling)

Money is a curious thing, isn't it, Richard?

RICHARD
(Small boy)

I don't know; I've never had too much.

JACK

No: the thing and the symbol. It's a piece of paper, with
ink on it . . . and the ink and the paper together aren't
worth a quarter of a cent—less . . . yet if we didn't have
it, the world would stop.

RICHARD

We could go back to barter.

JACK

Yes, I suppose we could. It's like painting. A stretch of
canvas and some paint. Worth what? Four dollars? Five?
Yet put a value on it. Let *me* do it, and it sells for a certain sum, or someone else, and ten times more . . . a
hundred! A certain Picasso for half a million? Not a
bad painting, *worth* it, maybe. Money. How much does
a cow sell for?

RICHARD

I don't know . . . two hundred dollars?

JACK

Maybe. Let's say. One Picasso painting for twenty-five
hundred cows. All that milk. How many gallons does a
cow give off in a day?

RICHARD

Fifteen?

JACK
(Some astonishment)

Gallons?

RICHARD

No. Quarts. I think I read it.

JACK

O.K. *(Figures in his head)* That comes to . . . fifteen times
twenty-five hundred is . . .

RICHARD

You want a pencil and paper?

JACK
(Figures; waves him off)

. . . figuring three hundred and *sixty* days a year, giving
the cows holidays off. Thirty-seven-five times thirty-six
and carry all those zeros . . . comes to . . . good God!
Thirteen and a half million quarts of milk in a year.

RICHARD

You're kidding!

JACK

No; I'm not. Thirteen million and a half quarts of milk
in one year.

RICHARD

That's incredible!

JACK

It is, isn't it. How much does milk go for wholesale?

RICHARD

Ten cents?

JACK

No, less. There's all that awful mark-up before it gets to
us. Let's say five cents. Thirteen-five by twenty . . . this is
even *more* fascinating! Nearly seven hundred thousand
dollars a year for the milk alone!

RICHARD

What are you getting at?

JACK

Which would YOU rather have? The Picasso or the cows?

RICHARD
(Thinks, shakes his head; genuine)
I don't know. Another drink?

JACK
(Gulps his down, simultaneously shaking his head)
No. I've got to get to the club. Old Digby's waiting, pant-ing at the backgammon board.

RICHARD
Oh. O.K.

JACK
(Both have risen; stops)
Now that's the *interesting* thing. Old Digby. Do you know that he's eighty-seven, by the way? He *adores* money . . . and not as a symbol . . . as a *thing* in itself. I'll bet he's got sixty million if he's got one, but it's all a *thing* with *him*. It doesn't become Picassos or cows or . . . anything but just the paper as paper. Money as money.

RICHARD
(Pause, almost apologetic)
Money *is* money, you know.

JACK
(Apologetic; gentle)
I *know* it is.

RICHARD
(Quietly dogmatic)
It's paying for this house, and a good education for Roger, and something every once in a while to make Jenny happy . . .

JACK

I *know; I know.*

RICHARD
(Indicates the money on the desk)
So, when something like *this* comes along . . . well, it
means something.

JACK

I wasn't making fun of you.

RICHARD

Don't tell Jenny, but I might be able to get her some kind
of greenhouse, a small one . . .

JACK

I told you: not a word about anything. Money? *What*
money? I've got to go. *(Starts out french doors)* It just
occurred to me that I don't think I've ever used the front
door in this place. Is it nice?

RICHARD

The front door?

JACK

Mmm.

RICHARD
(He'd never really thought about it before)
Well, *yes* . . . it's all right, I guess.

JACK

I must do it someday.

RICHARD

Jack?

(JACK *stops, half out*)

Nothing.

JACK
(*As* RICHARD *turns away; to the audience*)
He's *right;* and I *wasn't* making fun of him. Money . . .
is . . . money. See you. (*Exits*)

JENNY
(*Bounces back in*)
Are you two . . . ? Oh. Is Jack gone?

RICHARD

Um-hum.

JENNY
(*Sort of breathless*)
Chuck and Beryl are coming; they were going to just
sort of sit around; and I got Cynthia and Perry, or I got
Cynthia, rather, and they had to get out of something,
but they'll be here, too, and I'm trying Gil and Louise
but their line keeps being busy, so I'll go back and finish
that up.

RICHARD
O.K. You want a martini now?

JENNY
No; when I come back. (*As she goes again*) Roger should
be arriving soon. He'll have to take a taxi from the station.

RICHARD
A *taxi!?*

JENNY
(Pauses her flight momentarily)
Yes; a taxi. *(Indicates the money)* Don't you think we can
afford one?

RICHARD
(It sinks in; he laughs sheepishly)
Oh. Hunh! Yes, I guess we can.
(JENNY exits)
*(RICHARD looks at the money, straightens it out;
reaches in his pocket for a cigarette, finds none,
looks around for one. Finds a cigarette box
empty, looks some more)*

RICHARD
(Half calling)
Jenny, where did you put the cigarettes? Never mind, I
can find them.
*(Hands on hips for a moment, pondering. Goes
to—what? a side table, maybe—opens a
drawer, looks in, rummages, suddenly halts, fro-
zen. Puts his hand on something, slowly brings
it out. It is a bundle of money. He looks at it,
looks over to the pile on the table, looks back at
the money in his hand, drops the new bundle
down on a chair, or the sofa, whichever is
handier, and looks around the room, spies JEN-
NY's sewing basket—say—and goes over to it;
hesitates just a moment, then opens it, reaches
in, takes out yet another bundle of money
which he regards with a curious intensity as he
takes it over and dumps it down where he put
the last. Spies a box on the mantel and goes
to it, opens it, and comes up with a fistful of
money. He lets it fall, like confetti, all around
him)*

JENNY
(Re-enters)
Well, that's done. Gilbert and Louise are coming, too, so that makes . . . *(She stops, sees what he has found)* . . . everybody we asked.

RICHARD
(In a kind of a fog)
Jenny; look. What *is* it?

JENNY
Money, Richard.

RICHARD
But . . . is it . . . is it yours?

JENNY
There isn't time to tell you now, I . . .

RICHARD
Yes. There is. You must.

JENNY
We have so much to do before . . .

RICHARD
Wait! *(Points to the money on the table)* Did you send me that package?

JENNY
Actually, yes . . . well, I *had* to; there was *so* much, and I couldn't think of any way to . . .

RICHARD
Have you been . . . have you been *gambling*?

JENNY
(Jumping on that)

Yes!

RICHARD

Where? On what? Who through?

JENNY

There's . . . there's this man.

RICHARD

Called?

JENNY

What does it matter so long as I've been winning?

RICHARD
(Steelier)

Called?

JENNY

Desorio.

RICHARD

That's a lie.

JENNY

Don't you *talk* to me like that!

RICHARD

Isn't it a lie?

JENNY

Well . . . sort of.

RICHARD

THEN IT'S A LIE!

JENNY
(Shrugs)

Yes.

RICHARD

How much is there here? There's thousands!! Where did you get it?

JENNY
(Defensive)

I didn't *steal* it.

RICHARD
(Steely)

Where did you *get* it!?

JENNY

I earned it.

RICHARD

A job! You've got a job!

JENNY

Sort of.

RICHARD

I *told* you I didn't want you to take a *job*. No! You couldn't have earned this at a job. There's too much! There's thousands of dollars here, and . . .

JENNY

Six months!

RICHARD
(Laughs ruefully and half hysterically)
No, look, darling; look. Tell me. Did . . . did someone
leave it to you? Did someone die and you haven't told
me?

JENNY
Nobody died. I earned it. *(Slight pause)* In the afternoons.

RICHARD
Look; sweetheart: even if you worked full-*time* you
couldn't have earned *this* kind of money. Come on now;
tell me.

JENNY
(Miffed and playing for time)
Oh? Really? I guess *not* if all I'm supposed to be good
for is a domestic or something.

RICHARD
(Gritting his teeth)
Where did you *get* it?

JENNY
(Sighs, rattles it off)
I make two hundred dollars an afternoon, four days a
week, sometimes more. I've spent a little on clothes, but
there hasn't been time to *spend* the rest, and . . .

RICHARD
Nobody pays that sort of money! I mean you've no train-
ing.

JENNY
You don't *need* any.

RICHARD
(Bewildered, and getting angry at the mystery)
What *do* you need?

JENNY

Where's my martini? You promised me an ice-cold, su-
per-special . . .

RICHARD
(Grabs her arm)
Now tell me!

JENNY

Ow! Now let go of me!
*(He does; she rubs her arm as they glare at
each other. Subdued)*
There's nothing worth telling.

RICHARD

By God, you tell me or I'll make a bonfire of this money
in the middle of the lawn!

JENNY
(Pleading underneath)
Don't be ridiculous! It's money!

RICHARD

I want to know where it comes from!

JENNY
(Her voice rising, too)
It comes from a job!

RICHARD

What *kind* of a job!?

JENNY
(Wild hunting)

A . . . a receptionist.

RICHARD

For *that* kind of money? *(Snorts-sneers)*

JENNY

It's a very expensive place!

RICHARD

What *sort* of expensive place?!

JENNY

A . . . a doctor's office.

RICHARD

You expect me to believe you sit behind the desk at some god-damn doctor's office a couple of hours in the afternoon, and you get two hundred dollars a day for it?! You must think I'm crazy!!

JENNY

It's a very special and very expensive place!

RICHARD
(A little fearful, a little disgusted)

What, what is it, some kind of . . . of abortionist office, or something?

JENNY

My God, you're disgusting!

RICHARD

Why! I've read in the paper of a man found out his wife

worked for an abortionist, brought him patients, as a matter of fact.

JENNY

You're disgusting!!

RICHARD

Well, I'm *sorry;* but if you're going to be so damned secretive, what am I *supposed* to think? Hunh?

JENNY
(Trapped and furious)
Think what you like!! *(Quite cutting)* Don't you want the money?

RICHARD
(Both furious now)
The money's got nothing to do with it!

JENNY

Oh yes it has! You don't think I do it for pleasure, do you?

RICHARD

Do what!? Sit behind a desk!?

JENNY

Yes; sit behind a desk!

RICHARD

What's the name of this place?

JENNY
(Daring him)
No name; just a number.

RICHARD

Yeah? Well, what's the number?

JENNY

It's confidential!

RICHARD

I'm your husband!

JENNY

I'm your wife! Do you tell me everything?

RICHARD

I like being told the truth!

JENNY

How much do you talk about *your* job? To *me*.

RICHARD

It's a dull job!

JENNY

So's mine!

RICHARD

The money isn't! The money isn't so damn dull! Christ!
It's four times what *I* get. *(Contemptuous)* Sitting behind
the desk in a doctor's office . . . sounds more like a high-
class whorehouse!

JENNY

I don't *like* that word.

RICHARD

Whorehouse! Call house! Cat house!

(There is a silence. JENNY *looks out toward the garden.* RICHARD *begins to realize he's hit on it)*
No; look; come on; what is it *really?*

JENNY
(Looking away; sort of wistful, sad)
Just a place.

RICHARD
A place.

JENNY
Where they pay me.

RICHARD
(Grabs her arm again)
For God's sake! What do they pay me for!?

JENNY
It's *me* they *pay!* *(Long pause; sort of lost)* Don't you want the money?

RICHARD
(Lets go of her arm, backs away a little, shakes his head; stuttered, almost laughing disbelief)
I, I don't . . . I don't believe it. I, I don't believe it.

JENNY
(Quite light)
Then don't.

RICHARD
(Backs a bit further away; same confusion)
I, I can't *believe* it. I CAN'T.

JENNY
(Coming toward him; the nicest smile)
Darling, it's going to make such a tremendous difference.

RICHARD
(Laughing mirthlessly at the irony)
Oh, by God it is!

JENNY
(Still happy; occupied)
All the things we've been wanting for years . . .

RICHARD
We!

JENNY
We can have a second car, and . . .

RICHARD
There's no . . . I don't believe this!

JENNY
There's no what?

RICHARD
Room in the garage. *(Incredulous)* How could you *do*
such a thing!? *(Pause)* Come on, it *isn't* true, is it?
(JENNY nods, slowly)
No; is it? Really?

JENNY
(Dogmatic; impatient)
It is for *us;* for everything we *want!*

RICHARD
*(Between set teeth; quiet rage, letting it sink in
firmly)*
You are my wife; and Roger's mother; and you are a common *prostitute!?*

JENNY
That's a *horrid* way to *put* it.

RICHARD
HOW THE HELL AM I SUPPOSED TO PUT IT!!?

JENNY
I'm not the only *one*, you know. I'm not the only person in the world who . . .

RICHARD
You're the only one who's married to *me!*

JENNY
(Triste reasoning)
But it doesn't make any difference to *us*, and . . .

RICHARD
(Hard)
Doesn't it? *(Walks over to her, slaps her hard across the
face)* Doesn't it? How much do you charge for *that?* *(She
just stares at him, firm but maybe near tears way underneath. So he slaps her again, just as hard)* I said: how
much do you charge for that!!

JENNY
*(Says nothing, really, maybe a kind of growl-
cry as she slaps him back, just as hard as he hit
her)*

RICHARD
(Cold, after a moment's pause)
Get out. Pack up and get out of here.

JENNY
(Equally cold)

Where!

RICHARD
Anywhere! Or I will. No, by God, I won't! It's my house,
I paid for it. I stay here!

JENNY
(Curiously unemotional)
I can't ... just like that.

RICHARD

I said get out!

JENNY

A lot of things here are mine.

RICHARD

Take them! Take them!

JENNY
(Through her teeth)
You certainly don't expect me to get everything togeth-
er right now and ...

RICHARD

I'll send it after you! Just ... just get out!

JENNY

No, no, you wouldn't. I know *you:* you can never manage

anything like that. I'm the one who has to get the movers and arrange everything, and . . .

RICHARD

CRAP!!

JENNY

Well, it's perfectly true. When your aunt what's-her-name wanted her big, ugly breakfront back, you said you'd take care of it, and *weeks* went by and you didn't do a damn thing.

RICHARD
(Quietly, with controlled rage)
Get your things together and get out of this house!

JENNY
(Tired of it all)
Oh, don't be silly.

RICHARD
(Fury and disbelief)
Don't be *what!?*

JENNY
I said, don't be silly. Give me a cigarette.

RICHARD
You god-damn wanton bitch!

JENNY
I am *not* wanton! I told you: it's for the money! The money *you* don't make! The money we *need!* You think I get any enjoyment out of it?

RICHARD

Think!? I, I, I, I. I don't think anything! I *can't!* I'd
go stark raving mad if I thought! Men kill their wives
for this sort of thing!

JENNY
(Giggles)

Oh, darling . . .

RICHARD
(Mocked, becomes uncontrollable)

You don't think they do? *(Starts toward her with serious
intent)* Read the papers and find out! By God, read tomorrow's papers and find . . .
*(They are both stopped by the sound of the
front door slamming. ROGER enters, from the
hallway)*

ROGER

Hi! I took a taxi; do you have any money?

JENNY
(As if she'd forgotten all about him and is sorry)

Roger!

ROGER

The taxi driver says he wants five dollars over the fare
because it was such a long way.

RICHARD
(Fury turned on driver)

Oh, he does, does he? *Well,* I'll fix that son of a bitch.
*(RICHARD exits, maybe pushing ROGER to one
side as he goes)*

ROGER
(Looks at RICHARD's *exit, confused; back to*
JENNY; *genuine affection)*
Hi, Mom.

JENNY
(Embarrassed, but covering)
Darling! You're so . . . so terribly early.

ROGER
(Statement of fact)
The train was on *time*.

JENNY
(A little flustered)
Oh? Was it? Well, then . . . our clock must be slow.

ROGER
Must be. *(Goes to a chair, stands on its seat, looks out
through french windows over fence)* How's the tennis?

JENNY
What tennis?

ROGER
(Points)
At the club.
(Angry voices from outside front door)

JENNY
(Looks off apprehensively)
Oh, I . . . I don't pay much attention.

ROGER
Dad been playing? I hope the cab driver doesn't kill
him.

JENNY
(Calling off; worried)

Richard? *(To* ROGER*)* Get *down* off that before your
father sees you!

ROGER

O.K. . . . *(Jumps down; sees the money)* Wow! Is that
money?

JENNY
(Preoccupied, defensive)

Yes, now . . . just leave it be.

ROGER

What is it, the sweepstakes?

JENNY

Just . . . don't concern yourself, now.

ROGER

Can I have a bunch?

JENNY
(Sudden anger)

No! Now let it alone!

ROGER
(Hurt, some)

I'm sorry. *(Heavy-handed irony)* Gee, am *I* glad *I* came
home.

JENNY
(Apologetic)

Oh, Roger, darling, I'm . . .
*(*RICHARD *reappears, a little mussed)*

RICHARD
(Vengefulness and pride)
I hit him!

ROGER
(Shy)
Hi, Dad.

RICHARD
(To JENNY, since she caused it)
I hit the son of a bitch!

JENNY
(Quite rebuking)
Did you say hello to your son?

RICHARD
Hm?

ROGER
(Shy, pleased)
Hi.

RICHARD
(Really sees ROGER for the first time; sadness and pride)
Hi. (Back to JENNY; quiet fury and glee) I hit that son
of a bitch.

JENNY
(Quietly desperate)
Why!

RICHARD
Why!!? He wanted nine dollars. The bastard wanted the
regular fare and five dollars extra because . . .

JENNY

That is no reason to hit anyone!

RICHARD

WHO AM I SUPPOSED TO HIT! *(Less loud, but no less intense)* Who am I supposed to hit!

ROGER
(To fill a tiny silence)

How's the tennis, Dad?

RICHARD
(To ROGER*)*

What?

ROGER
(Intimidated)

Tennis. How is it?

RICHARD
(Confused)

I, I haven't . . . I, I, I, haven't played.

ROGER

Un huh . . .

JENNY

You'll get a lawsuit on us, you know.

RICHARD
(Deflated; embarrassed, even)

I only hit him on the shoulder. We . . . we just scuffled
a little.

JENNY
(Pause, disappointment and relief)

Oh.

RICHARD
(A sneer)

Not what I wanted to do.
(ROGER has gone up on the chair again)

ROGER

Wow! Right in the crotch!

RICHARD

Who! What!

JENNY

Roger, don't use words like that.

RICHARD
(Scoffs)

Oh, Jesus!

ROGER

Serve took a bad bounce, hit him right in the . . . what word shall I use?

RICHARD

Don't ask your mother, she's too ladylike. *(Realizes where ROGER is)* GET THE HELL OFF THE GOD-DAMNED FURNITURE.
(ROGER does so)

ROGER
(Subdued, unhappy)

Sorry.

RICHARD

You think we're made of money?

ROGER
(Defensive, indicates money all over)
It *looks* like it.
(This sets in an embarrassed silence)

RICHARD
(To change the subject)
Did you have a good term?

ROGER

All right.

RICHARD

What's your average? What did you end up with?

ROGER

C plus.

RICHARD

What did you start out?

ROGER

C plus.

RICHARD
(Bitter)
Keep it up: by the time you're eighteen we won't even be able to get you into an agricultural college!

JENNY

Be nice!

(RICHARD's mouth drops open, but he doesn't say anything)
Set the clock right.

RICHARD

It *is* right.

ROGER

It's twenty minutes slow.

RICHARD
(Furious)

Then you set it right!

JENNY

Richard!

RICHARD

Shut up!
(ROGER goes to the mantel clock, takes it down)

ROGER

What do I do?

RICHARD

Turn the knob; turn the god-damn knob!

JENNY

Richard, if you can't be . . .

RICHARD
(Between clenched teeth)

I told you to shut up! *(To* ROGER*)* No! Too far! That's tooo . . . DON'T TURN IT BACK. *(Disgust, takes the* *clock, none too gently, from* ROGER*)* Here; give me the god-damn clock. NEVER TURN IT BACK! Don't ever turn a clock back!

ROGER
(Flustered, confused)
I'm sorry, I ...

JENNY
Roger, darling, why don't you take your bag upstairs, and ...

RICHARD
(Concentrating, excessively, on the clock; to himself as well as ROGER*)*
You *never* turn a clock back; *never.*

JENNY
Why don't you go unpack?

ROGER
(Sullen)
O.K. You've got so much money, I don't see why you don't go *buy* a clock.

RICHARD
ALL RIGHT!

JENNY
Go unpack and then you can come down and *help* us.

ROGER
You want me to go upstairs, or would you rather I turned around and went right back to school?

RICHARD

GET UPSTAIRS!!

ROGER
(Under his breath)

Christ!

RICHARD

And don't say that!

ROGER
(Standing up to him)

Why not! YOU do! *(Exits)*
(Small silence. RICHARD hurls the clock down on the floor)

JENNY
(Calm, displeased)

That helps.

RICHARD
(Intense, pounding his chest with his fingers)

It helps *me!* ME!!

JENNY
(Closes her eyes for a moment; then all business)

I wish you'd make a list of what we need, what liquor we need.

RICHARD
(Stares at her; quietly)

Whore.

JENNY
(Ignores it)
We'll have champagne, but there are always some peo-
ple don't like it, and . . .

RICHARD
(Ibid.)
Whore!

JENNY
. . . and so you'd better check. If we're going to have
fresh caviar, and I think we should, then I've got to go
down to Blaustein's and get some . . .

RICHARD
(Ibid.)
Filthy, rotten, no-good little whore!

JENNY
(Quite savage)
Be quiet! You've got Roger in the house!

RICHARD
(Top of his voice)
I'VE GOT A ROTTEN, FILTHY WHORE IN THE HOUSE!

JENNY
(Tiny pause; continues quietly)
Now make a list. They'll be here in about an hour . . .

RICHARD
(Laughing in disbelief)
A party! We're going to have a party!

JENNY
(Level)

Yes; we are.

RICHARD
(The tears that finally come, tears of rage and despair, are incipient; we notice what is coming by a quivering in the voice)

What, what shall we do? Make the announcement? Break it to the neighborhood? Tell them to tell their friends where they can go to get it? Hunh?

JENNY

Make a list.

RICHARD

Hunh? Is that what we should do? Is it? Whore? *(Tears nearer now)*

JENNY

You can phone for the liquor, but we have to know what we need.

RICHARD
(Tears even nearer)

Or, or maybe they already know. Maybe . . . maybe Chuck and Perry and Gil . . . do they . . . do they know already?

JENNY

List.

RICHARD

L, l, list? We . . . all, all right, we need . . . *(Crying commences now)* v, v, v, vodka, and . . .

JENNY
(Gentle)

American or Russian?

RICHARD
(Looks up; pleading)

Both?

JENNY

Both, then.

RICHARD

. . . and . . . and . . . sc, sc, sc, scotch, and . . . bourbon,
and . . . *(Full crying now)* . . . and gin, and . . . gin,
and . . . gin, and . . . *(The word* gin *takes a long time
now, a long, broken word with gasps for breath and the
attempt to control the tears)* . . . g—i—i—i—n, and . . .
     (Final word, very long, broken, a long howl)
G———i———i———i———i———n———n———n———n.
          (Curtain falls slowly as the word continues)

GIRARD TRUST BANK

PHILADELPHIA AND SUBURBS

DATE _12 May_, 19___

When endorsing checks, please indicate your account number under your endorsement.

ACCOUNT NUMBER

1-55 1-902

NAME _Steve Zelott_

ADDRESS _825 S 4th_

CITY _P_ STATE _Penn_ ZIP CODE _19143_

1B261BMAY 12

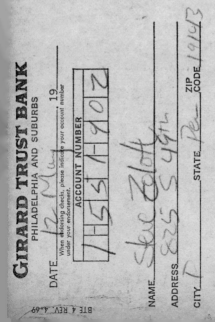

CUSTOMER'S COPY

This deposit is accepted subject to verification an the provisions of the uniform commercial code.

CHECKING ACCOUNT DEPOSIT

TOTAL CASH		00
LIST CHECKS	300	
1		
2		
3		
4		
5		
6		
7		
TOTAL	300	00

00 □□□□

BTE 4 REV. 4-69

ACT TWO

(Set the same; one hour later. RICHARD *alone on stage, sitting facing out at audience. It might be interesting if he looked the people in the audience right in the eye, but absently, seeing them, but thinking of something else. No attempt to set a new convention (with* RICHARD*), but it will give quite a few people an interesting sensation)*

> *(*JENNY *enters, followed by* ROGER*, both laden with glasses, etc.)*

JENNY
(Pleasantly incredulous)
What are you *doing?*

RICHARD
Hm?

JENNY
What are you *doing?* Roger, put those over there and be careful you don't break them.

ROGER
(Embarrassed at being warned)
O.K.

JENNY
(Puts her things down)
I asked you what you thought you were doing. You've got guests coming over in about ten minutes, and . . .

125

RICHARD
(Ugly but quiet; a threat of explosion)
What am I supposed to do?

ROGER
(Breaks a glass)
Damn!

JENNY
Oh, Roger . . .

RICHARD
That's right! Break the house up!

ROGER
It's only a glass, for God's sake, it . . .

RICHARD
We're not made . . . Do you know how much those things
cost?

ROGER
(Standing his ground)
No. How much?

RICHARD
(To JENNY*)*
How much do they cost?

JENNY
Well, they're new, and . . .

RICHARD
(Hint of hysteria; incipience)
They're new!?

JENNY
(Calm)

Yes, and they're crystal, and I suppose they . . . well, I
think they were about four-fifty each . . .

RICHARD
(After a pained look at JENNY; *to* ROGER, *shaking his head and sneering)*

Four-fifty each. You broke a god-damn glass and they
cost four . . .

ROGER
(Digs into his pocket)

Well, here. Take it out of this.

RICHARD
(Unpleasant joy)

Give it to your mother.

JENNY
(Laughing, covering)

Don't be silly, darling. No, Roger, no.

ROGER
(Hand out of pocket again)

Anything to keep peace in the house.

RICHARD

Don't be fresh!

JENNY
(Mollifying; to ROGER*)*

Darling, go upstairs and change. People *will* be here soon,
and I'll want you to help.

ROGER

Do I have to put on a tie?

RICHARD
(Furious)

Yes!

JENNY
(All on ROGER's side)

I'm afraid so, darling. Run along upstairs now.

RICHARD

Yes; *and* a shirt, *and* trousers, *and* socks, *and* shoes . . .

ROGER

Tie?

ROGER
(Going, shaking his head)

Wow.

RICHARD

And don't hang out the window watching the tennis. Change.

ROGER
(Sloppy salute)

Yes, sir! (Exits)

RICHARD

And don't salute!

JENNY
(After a tiny pause; reasonable, calm)

It was only a glass.

RICHARD
(Turns on her; quiet wrath)
What have you been doing: buying things behind my
back? Crystal? Gold goblets? Clothes?

JENNY
Just a little.

RICHARD
Just a little what!

JENNY
(Sighs)
A few clothes; those glasses; nicer sheets. Didn't you no-
tice?

RICHARD
(Still furious)
Notice what!

JENNY
(Quietly happy)
The nice sheets. I thought they'd . . .

RICHARD
No! I didn't notice the nicer sheets, and by God I won't
sleep on them! I won't sleep in the same room with you!

JENNY
(Cool)
And where are you going to sleep?

RICHARD
What?

JENNY

I said, where are you going to sleep? Roger's home, there's no mattress in the guestroom . . .

RICHARD

Why not! Where is it!

JENNY

You threw it out. When you had the hepatitis and you slept in there you said it was awful—the mattress— so we threw it out.

RICHARD

Well, why didn't we get another one!

JENNY
(Shrugs, starts arranging things)
Oh . . . money, or something.

RICHARD

WELL, WE CAN DAMN WELL AFFORD ONE NOW!

JENNY
(Quiet, precise)
I don't see the need. You've told me to get out.

RICHARD
(This stops him for the briefest instant only)
WELL, WHEN ARE YOU GOING!?

JENNY
(Stops what she is doing)
Right now. Right this very minute.

RICHARD

You've got a party! You've got people coming over!

JENNY
(Pretending this complicates things)
Oh. Yes. Well then, I'll leave right after the party, right
after everybody goes.

RICHARD
Fine.

JENNY
(Quietly withering)
Or shall I stay and clean up first?

RICHARD
(Can think of nothing for a moment, finally)
Tramp.

JENNY
There's no need for that now.

RICHARD
I can't hold my head up in front of those people; I won't
be able to look any of them in the eye. I might scream,
or cry, or something.

JENNY
You'll hold your head up. In fact, I should think you
might be *able* to look Chuck and Perry and Gil straight
in the eye, maybe for the first time.

RICHARD
Why! Because my wife is a whore?

JENNY
(Sort of cajoling)
No . . . well, because for once you won't be the poor
relative, so to speak; you can talk about the new car

you're going to get, and why don't we raise the dues at
the club to keep the riffraff out, and Jenny and I were
thinking about Antigua this winter—all those things.

RICHARD
(Some disgust)

You're hopelessly immoral.

JENNY

Not at all! I'm talking about money—that thing that keeps
us at each other's throats; that standard of judgment;
that measure of a man's worth!

RICHARD

There are other standards!

JENNY

Well, not in the circles *we* move in! Not in *our* environ-
ment.

RICHARD

There are *kinds* of money!

JENNY

Yes! Three! Too little, too much, and just enough!

RICHARD

Corrupt!

JENNY

Too much money corrupts; too little corrupts. Just
enough? Never.

RICHARD

It's how! *How!*

JENNY

Oh, don't tell me about how! Perry and that real estate
he sells? Ten thousand for an acre out near, uh, near
the track, and he doesn't even tell the god-damn fools
there isn't any city water? Gilbert and his fancy publish-
ing house? What's his advertising budget on trash? Thousands! How much does he spend on a halfway decent book
. . . nothing!

RICHARD

All right, all right . . .

JENNY

And you in your research laboratory. All those government contracts? A little work on germ gas maybe?

RICHARD

I told you that in . . . I told you not to say a word about
anything I told you . . .

JENNY

You told me in confidence? Well, I'm telling you *back* in
confidence! You all stink, you're all killers and whores.

RICHARD
(Nods several times rapidly)
That's quite a performance.

JENNY

You're damned right.

RICHARD
(Great sarcasm)
Bra-*vo!*

JENNY

At least! Come on! More!

RICHARD

With your theories on money, you should have married
Jack.

JENNY
(Self-mocking rue)

Unh-hunh; you may be right.

RICHARD

Though I don't necessarily think he'd take any better to
having a whore for a wife than I do.

JENNY
(Comforting)

Well, if I'd married Jack none of it would have happened.

RICHARD
(As ROGER *re-enters; starts to go for her)*

Why, you . . .

ROGER

I'm dressed.
(They both pause, for ROGER's *tone has a curious impersonal disapproval to it)*

JENNY
(Recovering)

And in good time, too. They'll start coming any second.
My, don't you look nice and grown-up.

ROGER

You've seen me in a tie before. *(To* RICHARD*)* Were you
going to hit her?

RICHARD

Mind your own business.

ROGER
(*Mildly puzzled*)

I thought it was.

RICHARD

Well, it's not. I don't suppose you washed.

ROGER

Well, I didn't have time for a sit-down bath, if that's what you mean. Why *isn't* it my business?

RICHARD

Because it isn't! Are your fingernails clean?

ROGER
(*To* JENNY, *the same mildly disapproving curiosity*)

Was he going to hit you? (*Looks at his nails*) Relatively.

JENNY

Don't be silly, darling; your father doesn't hit people bigger than he is. Come help me with things, now. Those glasses over there . . .

ROGER
(*Grumbling, sort of*)

People always hit each other when other people are out of the room.

JENNY
(*Decidedly offended*)

Roger!

RICHARD
(Snarl)

Little monster.

ROGER

I wasn't complaining; I was just stating a fact.

RICHARD

Keep your facts to yourself.

JENNY

Nobody hits anybody around here.

RICHARD

Anyway, not above the belt.

JENNY
("Not in front of Roger")

Richard!

RICHARD
(Subsiding)

Sorry! Very sorry. Sorry about everything. Every single thing.

ROGER
(An aside, to JENNY*)*

What's the matter with Dad?

JENNY
*(*RICHARD *can hear them both, of course)*

Oh, nothing; parties upset your father, that's all.

ROGER
(Goes to RICHARD: *genuine)*

I'll help.

RICHARD
*(Looks at him for a moment, then, with a head-
shaking laugh that could be confused with
mockery, but isn't)*
Oh, boy! Thanks!

ROGER
(Withdraws a little; stung)
I'm sorry.

RICHARD
(Quite furious)
Roger! I mean it! Thank you!

ROGER
(A little bewildered)
O.K.

(Doorbell rings)

JENNY
(Sighs, girds herself)
Well. Here we go.

RICHARD
(Little boy)
I'm going to hate this.

ROGER
Hey, what shall I drink?

RICHARD
Ginger ale.

ROGER
Awww.

JENNY
(Exiting)

I'll go.

RICHARD

Roger, do me a favor.

ROGER

Sure. What?

RICHARD

Grow up right.
(Sounds of greeting from hallway)

ROGER
(Offhand)

O.K. Got any ideas?

RICHARD

Just . . . be good.

ROGER

As the twig is bent, as they say.
(JENNY re-enters with CHUCK and BERYL)

BERYL
(To JENNY, as they enter)

No, it's been lovely, but I would love some rain. Our lawn is all brown and splotchy.

JENNY

Oh? Well, we manage ours.

BERYL

Green thumb, my darling.

CHUCK

Won't be any rain till we take off for . . . *Hel*lo, Richard!

RICHARD
(Shy)

Hi, Chuck; Beryl?

BERYL

Are we too early? I told Chuck we'd be first here.

JENNY

Don't be silly.

CHUCK

And I said, so what? First to come, last to leave; no breeding. Roger!

ROGER

Hello.

BERYL
(To ROGER; *some wonder)*

Do you grow each time I see you?

ROGER

Probably; I don't see you very much.

JENNY

He grows fresher each time you see him, I can tell you *that.*

CHUCK
(Formality)

How's school, Roger?

ROGER

Fine.

CHUCK

Back for vacation? Now, that's a silly question. Got any silly answers?

ROGER

I keep those for exams.
                    (Some laughter)

RICHARD

How true. Hey! How about a drink? Champagne or proper stuff?

CHUCK
(Hearty)

Champagne!

BERYL
(To CHUCK*)*

You know what it does. *(To* JENNY*)* Keeps him up all night; bent double. Gas?

CHUCK
(To RICHARD; *ruefully)*

I guess I better have some scotch.

RICHARD

Right. Beryl? *(Goes to her)*

ROGER

Can I help?

BERYL
(Examining caviar; to JENNY)
Fresh, how nice. Do you get yours in the city?

JENNY
No, Blaustein's has the fresh.

BERYL
(To RICHARD)
Gin, darling, and a little ice. *(Back to* JENNY) Well, fresh caviar can't keep, and I don't trust Blaustein's.

JENNY
(A tiny bit of pique)
Oh, it's perfectly fresh.

BERYL
(Slight laugh)
I'm sure it is. I just think Blaustein's cheats a little . . . keeps it on ice a day or two more than they . . .

JENNY
Would you like some caviar, Chuck?

CHUCK
Sure would. *(Goes to it)* Toast? Toast?

JENNY
No; crackers.

BERYL
(Moving away from caviar, looks at garden, expansive)
How do you keep it!? How do you battle the weeds, and prune and dust . . . ?

JENNY
(Proud)

Green *thumb*.

CHUCK

Cheers!

THE OTHERS
(Nearly simultaneously)

Cheers!

BERYL

While I've got you now, I need you for the blood bank.

JENNY

Richard can't.

BERYL

Why?

JENNY

Hepatitis. And Roger shouldn't, either; he needs all he's
got.

ROGER

I don't mind giving blood.

JENNY
(Light, but firm)

I don't think you *should*, Roger.

BERYL

Well, Jenny, then you'll have to give for the whole family.

RICHARD

I don't think she should.

BERYL

Why ever not?

JENNY

Yes. Why not?

RICHARD
(Dogmatic)

I just don't think you should.

JENNY
(A little annoyed)

Well, do you have a reason? Or are you just hoarding everybody's blood?

RICHARD
(Too much attempt at a joke; only JENNY *will see what he means)*

Well, no; you . . . you might have some awful disease for all *you* know.

BERYL
(As CHUCK *laughs)*

Oh, Richard! Really!

(Doorbell)

ROGER

Shall I go?

JENNY
(Exiting; a quick look at RICHARD*)*

I'll go. Help yourselves to the . . . *(Leaves it unfinished; exits)*

RICHARD
(The tiniest mockery)
How's high finance, Chuck? How's the old market?

CHUCK
Oh, just like marriage . . . up and down, up and down.
(BERYL and RICHARD laugh flimsily)

ROGER
What does *that* mean?

RICHARD
Nothing.

ROGER
Then why did he say it?

RICHARD
(Annoyed)
You know perfectly well what it means, so why did you
ask?

ROGER
(Shrugs)
I thought it was polite. You told me to help.
(JENNY re-enters, with GILBERT and LOUISE)

JENNY
Richard! It's Gilbert and Louise!

RICHARD
Well! Come on in! You know Beryl and Ch . . .

LOUISE
Yes, I think we've met at the club.

GILBERT

Yes, of course we have.

BERYL

How nice to see you both again.

CHUCK

Drinks are over here. There's champagne *and* the real stuff.

LOUISE

How nice you were to ask us. Oh, will you look at your garden! And the lawn! *How* do you do it?

BERYL

I was commenting before. I *don't* know how they do it.

GILBERT

Who's your gardener? Shropie?

RICHARD

Who?

GILBERT

Shropshire; he has a whole team, and . . .

JENNY

No, we've been doing it ourselves.

LOUISE

We have Shropshire, and they send two men, but we have six acres, too, so that makes a difference.

GILBERT

Charge an arm and a leg.

BERYL

But are they *good*. Chuck and I were thinking of using
them, and . . .

CHUCK

Not going to get me mowing weekends . . .

JENNY

It sort of spoils the fun to farm it out—the work . . .

RICHARD
(A little tentative)
We, we could have someone in, though.

JENNY
(Secret smile)
Oh? Well, why don't we?

RICHARD
(Bitter at being caught)
Spoils the fun.

JENNY
(To the others)
We thought we might put a greenhouse in, though.

RICHARD

Did we!

LOUISE

Oh, you must. We're so glad *we* did.

JENNY

I've always wanted one.

CHUCK

You must be in the chips, Richard old boy: greenhouse, champagne, caviar . . .

RICHARD
(Laughs lightly)

No; just . . . *(Shrugs, leaves it unfinished)*

JENNY

No, just not scrimping.

BERYL
(Her eyes narrowing slightly)

Oh, I'm glad.

ROGER
(Weary of asking)

Can I help?

LOUISE

Roger, *dear!* I didn't even say hello to you. Gilbert! Roger's here.

GILBERT

Roger, my boy. Home from school?

ROGER
(False heartiness)

Yes, Sir!

GILBERT

Doing O.K.?

ROGER

Holding my own, as they say.

GILBERT

Good boy; good boy. Hey, Rich; this is good caviar.
Where'd you get it?

RICHARD

Jenny got it; it's Jenny's.

JENNY

I got it at Blaustein's, just as fresh as if you'd gone into
town and . . .

GILBERT

Damn smart little kike, that Blaustein, putting in caviar
and . . .

ROGER

We don't use words like that around here.
    *(Everybody looks at him, not quite sure of
     what he means)*
At least, not in the family.
                    (Doorbell again)

JENNY
(Glad of the chance)

I'll get it! *(Exits)*

BERYL   LOUISE
    (Both just to say something)

I still say if you get it in The first year we had *our*
town it's bound to be fresh- greenhouse, I was amazed.
er.

RICHARD

Drinks now! Come on, kids; the bar's open.

GILBERT
(To RICHARD *as they approach the bar)*
What did I say?

RICHARD
Nothing, nothing.

CHUCK
Your kid's sort of a wise-acre, hunh?

GILBERT
(Hurt)
What did I say?

(Simultaneous)

RICHARD
Nothing; forget it.

BERYL
But aren't they a terrible chore?

CHUCK
I don't get the champagne. What for? What gives?

LOUISE
Well, no; not if you remember things, like water, and air, and heat, and . . .

(Simultaneous)

RICHARD
What gives? Nothing.

BERYL
(Laughs)
Ah, just a few things like that!

CHUCK
Looks pretty festive to me.

LOUISE
It takes getting used to, that's all.

ROGER
(If anyone cares)
I apologize.
*(*JENNY *re-enters, with* CYNTHIA *and* PERRY*)*

JENNY

The stragglers. Cynthia and Perry Straggler.

PERRY

Hi, folks.

ROGER
(To himself)

Folk.

GILBERT

Well, if it isn't old Perry! Hi, Cyn!

CYNTHIA
(Generally)

Hello there!

RICHARD

Bar's here, kids.

CYNTHIA

Well, will you look at all that!

CHUCK

Is it true what I heard, Perr?

PERRY

Probably. What?

CHUCK

You been selling lots to the black folk twice the going price?

(Some laughter, for this is a joke)

PERRY

Not a word of it! Three times the going price, and at that
I don't let 'em have clear title.
(More laughter)

ROGER

There are two Negro boys at school, on scholarship.

GILBERT
(None too pleasant)

Oh yeah? (To RICHARD) You ought to send your boy to
Choate, Dick. That's a *good* school.

ROGER

There are Negro boys there, too.

GILBERT

You're kidding.

ROGER

Why not? I mean, why am I kidding?

BERYL
(Not snobbish)

It *is* getting to be a problem.

CYNTHIA

I *know*.

LOUISE
(Very serious)

Well ... it's a time of change.

JENNY

It's time for a drink, that's what it's time for! Cynthia?
Louise?

ROGER

Actually, there won't be any solution to the color problem—whatever *that* is—until we're all coffee-colored.

BERYL

Roger!

JENNY

Darling!

GILBERT

Where'd you pick up *that* theory?

ROGER

A book.

PERRY

A little knowledge is a dangerous thing, Roger.

CHUCK

Theories that come out of books ought to stay in books.

RICHARD
(To ROGER)

Why don't you pass the caviar? I thought you wanted to
help.

ROGER

I've been *ask*ing! I've been standing around on my two
hind feet asking if I could be any help and everybody's
been ignoring me!

RICHARD
(Put out)

You've been standing around on your two hind feet in-

*sult*ing everybody, that's what you've been standing around
doing.

ROGER
(Something of a pout)

That was after.

CYNTHIA

Oh, let him alone, for heaven sake! He's a sweet boy.
How old are you, Roger, dear?

ROGER

I'm twelve.

JENNY

You're fourteen!

RICHARD

He *is* not; he's fifteen.

JENNY

I ought to know how old my own son is.

RICHARD

You ought; yes.

CHUCK

Where you going to put the greenhouse, Dick?

RICHARD

Hm? Oh . . . out there. *(Gestures vaguely)*

JENNY
(Rather pointed)

Show them *where*, darling.

RICHARD
(Trapped)

Hm?

LOUISE

Oh, I'd love to see! Show us!

CYNTHIA

Yes! And I want to look at Jenny's roses.
(CYNTHIA and LOUISE start out through french
doors; PERRY automatically follows)

CHUCK

Well, into the garden we go. Somebody bring a bottle of
champagne.

GILBERT
(Following CHUCK)

Nobody's drinking champagne.

CHUCK

Well . . . bring a bottle of scotch.
(The two men laugh, follow the others out)

JENNY
(To RICHARD)

Well . . . ?

RICHARD
(Getting it straight)

Show them where we're going to put the greenhouse.

JENNY
(Dazzling if mirthless smile)

Yes.

(Doorbell rings: JENNY starts)

Who's that? We didn't ask anyone else.

RICHARD
(Exiting to garden)

It's your party; you figure it out.

JENNY
(To BERYL)

I can't imagine who it is. Roger, darling . . . go see.
(ROGER exits through archway)
Unless it's Jack Foster. He always drops in, and . . .

BERYL
(Starts exiting to garden)

Well, if it is, I'll leave the two of you alone.

JENNY
(Annoyance showing through)

And what is that meant to mean!

BERYL
(Throaty laugh, as she exits)

Nothing, darling; nothing at all.
*(We will probably see one or more of the people
out in the garden while they admire it and
while RICHARD improvises where the greenhouse
will be, but their backs will be to us, and they
will not see inside until they return.)*

ROGER
(Re-entering)

It's a woman to see you.
*(MRS. TOOTHE enters; JENNY stares at her,
openmouthed)*

MRS. TOOTHE

Good evening, my dear.

(JENNY *just stares*)

I said, good evening, my dear.

JENNY

(Still staring at her)

Roger, go in the garden.

ROGER

(Bland)

Why?

JENNY

(Turns, snaps)

I said go in the garden!

ROGER

(Some disgust, turns on his heel, goes)

Good God!

JENNY

(Appalled)

What do you want?

MRS. TOOTHE

I want to talk. *(Sits)* Ah! That feels good. I do so hate to
walk.

JENNY

You can't *come* here; you *must*n't.

MRS. TOOTHE

I know, my dear, it's very indiscreet, but most important.

JENNY
(Anger, and panic underneath)
I'm having a party! Guests!

MRS. TOOTHE
Yes, I see; fine, I'm one of them.

JENNY
No! I'm sorry; no!

MRS. TOOTHE
Why not?

JENNY
They're friends; Richard thinks you're on the hospital committee, and . . .

MRS. TOOTHE
Fine, I'm on the hospital committee.

JENNY
But these are local people, and Beryl is on the hospital committee, and . . .

MRS. TOOTHE
Beryl?

JENNY
Yes, and Louise is too . . . and, and . . .

MRS. TOOTHE
Well, you'll just have to make up something: I'm not from *here*, I'm from . . .

JENNY

Please! Leave!

MRS. TOOTHE
(Firm, coldly polite)

I told you, my dear, it's a matter of considerable impor-
tance. Does your husband know?

JENNY

Yes, I told him today. Oh, my God, if he sees you and
knows who you are, I don't know what he'll . . .

MRS. TOOTHE

Well, he will have to make the best of it. *(Pause, smile)*
Will he not?

JENNY
(The final supplication of her life)

Please! *Please* leave!
              (BERYL and CHUCK have started back in)

MRS. TOOTHE

Your guests are coming back.
              (JENNY wheels)

BERYL
(Not noticing MRS. TOOTHE yet)

Jenny, my dear, Chuck and I agree: your husband is an
angel; the greenhouse will be absolutely perfect; you'll . . .

JENNY
(Cutting in)

Beryl, Chuck, this is Mrs. Toothe; Richard and I met her
down in St. Thomas last year, and she's come by to
say . . .

MRS. TOOTHE
(Quiet smile)
Hello, Beryl, my dear; I have a bone to pick with you.

CHUCK
(As JENNY watches, openmouthed)
My God, what's she doing here?

BERYL
(Cool, calm)
Oh? You have?

MRS. TOOTHE
Yes; indeed I have.

JENNY
(Finally, to BERYL, flabbergasted)
You!?

BERYL
*(As MRS. TOOTHE chuckles some, quite calm,
with a tiny smile)*
Yes; and you, too, it would seem.

JENNY
(Awe)
My God.
*(The others are coming in now, LOUISE, CYN-
THIA, PERRY, GILBERT and RICHARD; ROGER is
still outdoors)*

LOUISE
. . . and it seems to me that if you want the afternoon
sun, well, then you'll have to make allowance for it,
and . . . *(Sees MRS. TOOTHE)*

RICHARD
(All have seen MRS. TOOTHE *save* RICHARD; *all
are staring at her save him)*
It *could* be swung about, I suppose, though we'd have
to dig up someth—*(He sees her, sees the silence; to* MRS.
TOOTHE*)* Hello; I've seen you before, haven't I?

MRS. TOOTHE
(Very nice)
Yes, but we didn't really meet; I'm Mrs. Toothe. Hello,
Cynthia; Louise, my dear.
(They nod)

RICHARD
(Not getting it yet)
Well, then, you all know each other, and . . .

MRS. TOOTHE
Where were you on Thursday, Beryl dear?

BERYL
I had, I had a headache, and . . .

MRS. TOOTHE
Well, that will cost you a hundred dollars. Someone was
disappointed.

RICHARD
(Not quite dawn yet)
You, you all know each other?

MRS. TOOTHE
Well, yes, I know all these ladies, and I've met their husbands, but I've known them, well, how shall I say . . . I

don't think we've all known before that we all know each
other.

JENNY
(Lame and unhappy)
This is . . . Mrs. Toothe, darling.

GILBERT
(Rather pleased)
Perry, you never told me.

LOUISE
Cynthia, dear, I'm surprised we haven't run into each
other in town.

RICHARD
(Piecing it together)
Look, now, does this mean . . .

PERRY
(He, too, rather pleased)
Well, my God.

MRS. TOOTHE
(To RICHARD)
And isn't it charming that all my suburban ladies should
be under one roof.

RICHARD
All your ladies, and . . . *(To the women) All of you? (To
the men)* And *you've* known about it?

GILBERT
(Not quite pleasant)
Well, of course.

PERRY
(Slightly condescending)
Yes; naturally.

BERYL
But how absolutely marvelous none of us has known
about the other.

CYNTHIA
(To LOUISE: *mock chiding)*
You and your shopping trips.

LOUISE
(Giggles a little; to BERYL*)*
And all that museum-going.

MRS. TOOTHE
(Businesslike)
Well. Here we all are.

RICHARD
*(Backing off a little; quietly, as if facing a wall
    of strange shapes)*
I don't believe it, I . . . I don't believe it, I . . .

JENNY
(Quietly pleading)
. . . Richard . . .

CHUCK
(Shakes his head, chuckles)
Oh, boy! Oh, Jesus Christ! *(Full laughter)*

RICHARD
(To PERRY*)*
You've . . . you've known? All the time?

GILBERT
(Slightly patronizing)
What did you do, just find out?

RICHARD
(Tiny pause, a real scream)
YES!!!!

(Pause)

CHUCK
(Calm, fairly stern)
Get yourself a drink, boy. Quiet down.
(CHUCK pats RICHARD on the shoulder, makes for the bar)

RICHARD
(Softer; great loss in it now)
Yes!

GILBERT
(Matter-of-fact)
Well, now you know; and now we all know.
(ROGER enters)

ROGER
Hi! You know, Venus is up already? The sun isn't even down yet, and . . .

JENNY
Roger; go get something.

ROGER
M-m'am?

JENNY
Richard? *Do* something?

PERRY
(Digs into his pocket)
Roger, be a good fellow and run over to the club and
get me some pipe tobacco, will you?

ROGER
(Senses the silence)
Well . . . sure.

PERRY
And get yourself a Coke, or something.

JENNY
That's a good boy.

ROGER
(Puzzled, slightly reluctant)
O.K. . . . what, what kind?

PERRY
What?

ROGER
What kind of *pipe* tobacco?

PERRY
Ben at the desk; Ben knows; tell him it's for me.

ROGER
(Suspicion, confusion over, bounds out)
O.K. Be back!

RICHARD
Please, all of you, get out.

MRS. TOOTHE

As I said, I'm sorry I've had to come, but there's been trouble.

BERYL

What kind of trouble?

MRS. TOOTHE

So that I daren't use the phone; daren't call you.

PERRY

Police?

MRS. TOOTHE

Yes.

JENNY
(Quiet panic)

Oh, my God.

MRS. TOOTHE

A man named Lurie; detective, I think.

CHUCK

Can't you buy him off?

MRS. TOOTHE

Won't be had.

GILBERT

That's damned odd.

MRS. TOOTHE

Yes; well; nonetheless, he won't.
(RICHARD *watches all of this from a distance; maybe sits*)

PERRY

Asking questions?

MRS. TOOTHE

No ... telling me to clear out.

LOUISE

He didn't ask for *names*.

MRS. TOOTHE

It wasn't a *raid*. Besides, he wouldn't get them.

BERYL
(Sighs with relief)

Well.

GILBERT

Yes; there is *that*.

MRS. TOOTHE
(Brightly)

I don't believe I've been asked what I would like to
drink. *(Pause) Have* I?

JENNY
(Quite preoccupied, mostly with what RICHARD *is
thinking)*

Oh, no; I don't guess you have.

MRS. TOOTHE
(To RICHARD)

Unless you have an objection to my ... wetting my lips
in your house.

RICHARD
(Almost a monotone; a stunned quality)
No, you go right ahead; have what you like; there's champagne, and . . .

MRS. TOOTHE
(A little laugh)
Oh, heavens, no, I don't think so. *(To* CHUCK, *who is still near the bar)* Is there whiskey?

CHUCK
Sure. Neat?

MRS. TOOTHE
Very, and one cube.

CHUCK
No sooner said. *(To* RICHARD; *an afterthought)* O.K. if I . . . do the honors?

RICHARD
(As above)
No, you go right ahead.

CYNTHIA
I think I'd like one, too. Perry?

PERRY
Right.
(Some general movement to refill, hand drinks, etc.)

GILBERT
(To MRS. TOOTHE; *asking more than just his question)*
I . . . I suppose you'll have to . . . move out.

MRS. TOOTHE

I'm gone! I've left already. There'll be a psychiatrist
moving in.

BERYL
(Giggles)

That'll be a surprise for the regulars.

CYNTHIA
(Laughing, too)

Oh, Beryl! Really!

PERRY
(Stretching, breathing out)

Well, I guess you'd better hold off on that greenhouse,
Dick.

CYNTHIA

Yes, and put away the caviar.

LOUISE

What a shame. *(Afterthought)* What a shame for all of
us!

RICHARD
(Barely registering)

Hm?

GILBERT
(Fairly sententious)

Yes . . . things are going to be a little harder for *all* of us.

MRS. TOOTHE
(Sipping her drink)

Why? *(Good spirits)* This sort of thing happens. It's never
the end.

BERYL

It's rather different for you: you're used to it.

MRS. TOOTHE
(Speculative)

Ohhhh, one can get used to anything . . . I should say.
(To RICHARD*)* Wouldn't you say?

RICHARD

Oh, God.

LOUISE

Yes, but one can't get used to the idea of jail, not to men-
tion the newspapers and . . .

CHUCK

Cops are on to you.

PERRY

Where will you go?

MRS. TOOTHE
(Tiniest pause)

Why not . . . out here?

SEVERAL
(Tones of shock, disbelief)

Out here!

MRS. TOOTHE

Why not?

LOUISE
(Quite grand)

Surely you're not serious.

MRS. TOOTHE

Very good train service; respectable . . . countryside . . .

CHUCK
(Not sure)

Yes, there's very good train service, but . . .

MRS. TOOTHE

If one could find some suitable property. *(Looks at*
PERRY*)* Do you think?

PERRY

No, no, this wouldn't do at all . . .

GILBERT

Absolutely not.

MRS. TOOTHE
(Makes as if to get up and go; very businesslike)

Well, then; I shall just have to find a more congenial
city; somewhere where the police are fast asleep or . . .
amenable. I shall miss you ladies, though.

BERYL
(Tentative)

Of course . . . *(Stops)*

PERRY, CYNTHIA, GILBERT
(More or less simultaneously)

Yes?

BERYL
*(A little embarrassed, and pleased by the atten-
tion)*

Well, I was going to say . . . it . . . it couldn't be right
here: I mean right *here:* it could be . . . nearby.

JENNY
(She hasn't spoken for quite a while)
Well, *yes;* it would be . . . *(Leaves it unfinished)*

RICHARD
(As if hearing through fog)
What did you say, Jenny?

JENNY
*(Naked and embarrassed, but if you're in a
nudist colony . . .)*
I was going to say . . .

RICHARD
Yes. Go on.

JENNY
(If JENNY *can physically blush, yet be resolute, fine)*
I was going to say that if it could be out here then . . .
then it would be handy.

RICHARD
What was that last word?

JENNY
(Tiniest pause)
Handy . . . it would be handy.

RICHARD
(Nods, chuckles)
Um-hum. Oh, yes. *(Chuckles some more)* Oh, God, yes.
(A few defeated tears in the words) Especially with Roger
home: you could make it back and do the jelly sand-

wiches——now that he's not going to camp, 'cause we want
him here, not 'cause we can't afford it.

MRS. TOOTHE

I think we'd best keep this to a business discussion. Don't
you think?

PERRY

Yes; I think.

CHUCK

Good idea.

MRS. TOOTHE

Something to be talked about amongst us men. Jenny,
why don't you go out and show the girls your roses?

JENNY
(Occupied with observing RICHARD)

Hm?

MRS. TOOTHE

Show the girls your roses.

BERYL
(Leading the way)

Yes, why don't we see the garden again? There's so much
there; so very much to see.

CYNTHIA

Yes; coming, Louise?

LOUISE
(Gravely approving the proposition)

Of course.

MRS. TOOTHE

Jenny?

JENNY
(Loath to leave RICHARD, but going)
Well, all right . . . I . . . all right. *(Exits)*
(The men are left now, with MRS. TOOTHE)

RICHARD
(From where he sits; little emotion)
You're a little high-handed, aren't you?

MRS. TOOTHE
(Cheerfully soothing)
It's so much easier without them.

RICHARD

This *is* my house.

GILBERT

Oh, come off it, Richard.

CHUCK

We're lucky we're not all in jail.

MRS. TOOTHE

No, it won't come to that. Who will give me another
drink?

PERRY
(Takes her glass)
Whiskey and ice?

MRS. TOOTHE
Yes. *Thank* you. *One* cube.

GILBERT
(To CHUCK)
How much do you stand to lose?

CHUCK
(Rueful laugh)
Too *much;* damn *far* too much.

GILBERT
(Mulling)
Yeeesss. Tax-free? Be able to retire early if you wanted
to? If it kept up? Louise and I talked it over.

RICHARD
(Coming in, now; a neophyte)
You did? You talked it over? Just . . . talked it over?

GILBERT
Of course. Oh, I know how you *feel;* I felt that way . . .
for a little.

CHUCK
Wanted to break the *place* up.

PERRY
(Returning with MRS. TOOTHE's *drink)*
I *did* break the place up. Gave us an excuse to redecorate.

CHUCK
(Settling)
Funny how quickly you get used to the idea.

PERRY
Yes.

CHUCK

And, there *is* the money.

GILBERT

It's going to be a little tough to manage without it . . .
now.

PERRY

I can't take Martin away from his school at *this* stage . . .

GILBERT

Same with Jeremy; and there's Jennifer's pony. I'm paying through the nose to keep it at that damn stable, but I
can't sell it . . . she'd *kill* me.

CHUCK
(Fairly grim)
Anybody want to buy a nearly paid-for Aston-Martin?

PERRY

That's the trouble: we're all involved in things. We can't
. . . just stop.

GILBERT

And just between us, I don't mind admitting Louise and I
get along together much better these days.

PERRY

So do Cyn and I. Most of our arguments were over
money.

CHUCK

Yes.

MRS. TOOTHE
(To RICHARD)
Do you begin to understand better now?

RICHARD
(Still rather numb)
Oh yes; *I* understand.

MRS. TOOTHE
(Hears the women talking in the garden)
Listen to them. The girls chattering away.

PERRY
(Smiles)
Yes.

MRS. TOOTHE
Shall we talk business?

GILBERT
Right! Richard? Will you be chairman?

RICHARD
(A haze)
Will I what?

GILBERT
Be chairman. We want a proper business meeting.

CHUCK
(Moving in)
Here you are. Besides, it's your chair.

GILBERT
Who will propose him?

CHUCK
I.

PERRY

Seconded.

GILBERT

Carried.

CHUCK

Call the meeting to order, Richard.

RICHARD
(Brief hesitation, then)
Meeting come to order. *(Pause)* Well?

PERRY

Mr. Chairman, there *is* a property in our office that might
suit Mrs. Toothe's needs, and ours, very well indeed.

GILBERT

Not *here*.

PERRY

No; two stops up. Big house, pretty cheap, too: it's only
a couple of minutes' walk from the station.

MRS. TOOTHE

Sounds very good. How many rooms?

RICHARD

How many bedrooms, you mean, don't you?

MRS. TOOTHE

Will you be quiet! *(Back to normal tone)* If the price is
reasonable . . .

PERRY

Thirty-six.

MRS. TOOTHE

Twenty-eight. Yes, that will be all right. I shall look at
it tomorrow. I don't want there to be too much of a gap
in ... *(Smiles)* our services.

(RICHARD snorts)

Look here: I've spent time, and money, and energy
building up this enterprise, with a first-class clientele
and ...

RICHARD
(Mumbled)

All right, all right, all right ...

MRS. TOOTHE

Well, are there any questions?

CHUCK
(Satisfied)

Fine.

GILBERT

Seems good.

MRS. TOOTHE
(To RICHARD; none too pleasant)

You?

RICHARD
(Again, an attempt at sarcasm)

Oh, a couple.

MRS. TOOTHE
(Impatient, but not hurried)

Well, let us have them.

CHUCK
(Chiding)

Oh, Dick . . .

RICHARD

Doesn't it seem to bother any of you . . . Christ, every-body's going to know! Inside of two weeks it'll be all over the . . . doesn't that *disturb* any of you?

MRS. TOOTHE

We don't advertise in the local paper.

RICHARD

There's a thing called word-of-mouth.

MRS. TOOTHE

Your wives will know if there is any danger. Believe me . . . I know what I'm doing.

RICHARD

There's such a thing as messing on your own doorstep, isn't there?

GILBERT

That's a pretty rotten thing to say.

RICHARD

True.

GILBERT

Any other business?

CHUCK
(Guesses)

No . . .

PERRY

No ...

RICHARD
(Heavy sarcasm)
Well, in that case, I declare the meeting closed.

MRS. TOOTHE
There is one other thing ...

GILBERT

Mm?

PERRY

What is *that*?

MRS. TOOTHE
It's important that you carry on normally. You shouldn't talk about all this any more. I mean, even among yourselves.

GILBERT
We should forget it, you mean.

PERRY
Yes. We should forget it.

CHUCK

Quite right.

RICHARD
(A little quivering laugh—rage in this)
I don't quite see how we can ... just forget it.

MRS. TOOTHE
(Wise counsel)

Oh, yes you can. One can forget. If something isn't good to live with, or convenient, one can forget. After all, there are things you *have* to forget if you want to live at all.

RICHARD

Yes, but . . .

MRS. TOOTHE

But you all know this. You're men of family and education. You're not fools.

CHUCK

No; of course we're not.

PERRY

Quite right.

MRS. TOOTHE
(Rises, moves toward garden)

I think I'll go collect my ladies. *(Stops; to* RICHARD*)* One other thing for you to remember—one thing which might help you forget; two things: we do nobody any harm . . .

RICHARD

And the other?

MRS. TOOTHE

There's very little chance your wife will ever take a lover behind your back. *(She exits)*

GILBERT
(After a small pause)

Well, then; it's all set.

CHUCK
(Going to the bar)

Shall we drink on it?

PERRY
(Raises his glass)

Yes; here's to us.

GILBERT

To us. *(Notices* RICHARD *is just looking at his glass)*
Richard? To us? To all of us?

RICHARD
(Pause, self-deprecating little laugh; raises glass)

Sure; to us.

GILBERT
(Older brother)

You'll be all *right,* old man; you will be.

CHUCK AND PERRY
(Softly)

Cheers.

RICHARD
(Little boy; something lost)

Cheers.

(The ladies start coming back in)

BERYL

I find it quite hopeless to try to grow azaleas here, and
I don't know why.

JENNY

It's the lime in the soil, I think, but you can take care of
that.

BERYL

Ah, well; your thumb.

MRS. TOOTHE

Who will tend my garden? Are there local people?

CHUCK

Yes, good ones . . . but expensive.

MRS. TOOTHE

Ah, well, there will be enough . . . if everything works
out. Jenny, dear, may I use your telephone?

JENNY

Of course; let me show you.
                    (JENNY *and* MRS. TOOTHE *exit*)

BERYL

Well, let us ladies all have another drink, and then we
must go. It's all arranged, I understand.

CHUCK
                    (Moving to the bar)
I'll do the honors. Yes; all fixed.

PERRY

Perfect set-up.

LOUISE

Fine.

CYNTHIA

I couldn't be happier.

BERYL

Richard, no one is drinking your champagne, what a
shame; but I *will* have some of your caviar, crackers and
all.

RICHARD
(Sarcasm intended)

The champagne will keep; perhaps we can use it to
christen Mrs. Toothe's new house.
(General laughter as response; sarcasm not seen)

CYNTHIA
(Giggling)

Oh, Richard; really!
(JENNY returns)

JENNY

What did I miss?

LOUISE
(Her laughter dying)
Oh, nothing; Richard said something funny.

JENNY
(Relieved)
Oh. How very nice.
*(ROGER and JACK appear in the doorway to the
garden; JACK is quite drunk, but, even so, he
is exaggerating it)*

JACK

Hullo! Hullo! The gate-crasher is here; say hullo to the
gate-crasher. Say hullo to the gate-crasher. Say hullo!
*(They all turn, look at JACK; complete silence
from them)*

ROGER
(Giving tobacco to PERRY*)*
Here's your tobacco; I hope it's right.

JACK
Young Roger found me by the club; well, *at* it, actually;
at the club, and *at* the bar.

BERYL
(Cool)
That's rather evident.

JACK
Ooohhh, *honestly,* Beryl! *(Generally again)* Annnddd so,
I said to old Roger, how's the party, an' he told me, but
I thought I'd come anyway. And here I am, and all my
old friends, and isn't it wonderful.

JENNY
(Uncomfortable)
I . . . I thought you had a game, or something.

JACK
Backgammon with old Digby . . . well, old Digby died;
yes he did. Farnum was kneading away at him on the old
massage table, finished up, slapped him gently on the ass
and said, "All done, Mr. Digby, sir," and he just lay
there. Died horizontal on a metal board, which is as
splendid a way as any. Got the good vod out, Richard?
Got it hidden?

PERRY
(As JACK *makes for the bar)*
Go easy on the vodka, Jack.

JACK
(A dare)
Your house? Your vodka?

PERRY
No; but, still . . .

JACK
Tell you what I'll do, Perr, old thing: next time you
give a garden-type party, and I come unasked—which is
the only way I'll make it, if old Cyn has anything to say
about it, eh, kid?—*then* . . . I will go easy on the vod.
O.K.?

LOUISE
Do you, uh . . . do you bring any *other* charming news
from the club with you, dear Jack?

JACK
Anything other than poor old Digby? Weeellll . . . Oh!
Yeah! They got rid of Harry Burns.

GILBERT
Got rid of him? How?

JACK
Dug back—someone did; found out it was short for Bernstein; asked him to go.

CHUCK
(Disbelief, but not offended)
Oh, come *on*.

JACK
True; true.

LOUISE
(To BERYL*)*

Is Monica Burns *Jewish?*

BERYL

Well; I *suppose.*

LOUISE
(Some wonder)

I never would have *thought.*

CYNTHIA

She never let *on.*

LOUISE

Can you *imagine.*

JACK

For God's sake, you'd think she was a common prostitute, or something.
(Small silence)

BERYL
(Cold)

A what?

JACK
(Wagging his head)

A prostitootsie.
(Another small silence)

CYNTHIA

I can't say that Harry and Monica look . . .

LOUISE

No, no, they don't . . .

BERYL

Funny how you can sort of know, though . . .

JACK

After the fact, you mean.

PERRY
(Wincing a little)

Threw him out of the club?

ROGER

Some people say we're *all* Jews.

JENNY
(Not offended; startled)

What?

ROGER

The ten lost tribes.

GILBERT

Some people will say anything.

ROGER

And quite a lot of us are circumcised.
(Silence, save JACK, *who laughs softly)*

RICHARD
(Short, cold)

Go to your room.

ROGER

What?

RICHARD

Go to your room!

ROGER

Why!?

JENNY

He didn't mean to say anything.

ROGER

What did I say?

RICHARD

I told you to go to your room!

ROGER
(Standing his ground)

I want to know what I said wrong!

RICHARD
(Feeling foolish; this, though, merely pushes him further)

Don't you stand there and defy *me!!*

ROGER

It's not fair! You say much worse things!

RICHARD

I am your father and I tell you to go to your room. You're not fit to associate with decent people.

JACK
(Laughing, but serious)

Oh, come on, Richard!

RICHARD
(To JACK*)*

SHUT YOUR MOUTH! This is my house and my son! I tell him what to do! *(To* ROGER*) Go on!*

ROGER
(Supplication to the rest of the group)
But it comes up all the time in the Bible.

RICHARD
So do the Ten Commandments. Do you know the Ten
Commandments?

ROGER
Yes.

RICHARD
Say them.

ROGER
Now?

JENNY
Darling . . .

RICHARD
(Wheeling on her)
Leave me something! *(To* ROGER*)* Now!

ROGER
Thou shalt not kill.

RICHARD
That's one. Go on.

ROGER
(Looks to JENNY *for help, but there is none there)*
Thou shalt not . . . *(Falters)*

RICHARD
(To them all)

There; and a liar as well. Go up to your room.
(ROGER pauses, gives up, turns, begins going, shaking his head)

JACK

The poor bastard didn't say anything.

RICHARD
(Following ROGER)

Are you going to go to your room, or am I going to have to take you UP there?

JENNY
(To RICHARD)

Darling, let him . . . let him go out, or something. Let him go to the club. Just . . . *(Between her teeth)* . . . get him *out* of here.

RICHARD
(Sighs)

Oh . . . all right. *(Exiting, calling after ROGER)* Roger? Roger?

BERYL

They do need discipline.

GILBERT

A few licks with a belt from his father never did a boy any harm.

PERRY

Mine kept a riding crop.

GILBERT

And you never resented it, did you?

PERRY
(Can't recall)

I . . . I guess not.

JACK

How savage you all are today. Savage . . . and strange. All embarrassed, and snapping. Have I caught you at something?

BERYL

What do you mean!

JACK
(To audience)

Is there something going on here?

CHUCK

Have another drink, Jack.

JENNY

Yes! Let's everybody! Perry?
(General agreement and movement)

JACK
(Grabbing JENNY by the arm as she moves by him)

Jenny, my darling! Why do you all hate me? Why are you all trying to get me drunk?

JENNY
(Artificial little laugh)

Jack!

JACK

What's going on, Jenny?

JENNY
(Transparently lying)
Nothing, Jack. Nothing at all.

JACK

Do you still love me, Jenny?

JENNY
(Soothing the little boy)
Yes, Jack; of course.
(RICHARD re-enters)

JACK

Ah! Thank God! *(Rises)* Kiss and make up. *(He kisses her)*

RICHARD

I sent him out for a . . . What do you think you're doing!

JACK

I am kissing your beautiful wife.

RICHARD

Then stop it!

JACK

I *have* stopped.

RICHARD

I don't care for that sort of behavior.

JACK

Oh, come on, Richard. It might have been anyone. Hasn't
Jenny been kissed before?

RICHARD

You are not to kiss her!!

JACK

What is the *matter* with all of you this evening?

BERYL

There is *nothing* the matter with us.

JACK

There is something . . . very wrong.
                    (MRS. TOOTHE *re-enters*)

MRS. TOOTHE

Well, my dear children, my flock, I have made the necessary calls, and I think we . . . *(Sees* JACK*)* Ah. *(Her
eyes move from one person to another quickly)* I, uh . . .
I do believe we've met before.

JENNY
(Jumping in)

Jack, you *do* remember Mrs. Toothe; you met her . . .
oh, six-seven months ago, and . . .

JACK
(Staring at MRS. TOOTHE*)*

Yes; your fairy godmother.

MRS. TOOTHE
(To JACK; *very naturally)*

How nice to see you again.

JACK

How nice to see you. *(Turns away, thinking)*

MRS. TOOTHE
(To the others)

I *do* think I should be off now. It was so nice meeting you all . . .

JACK
(Suddenly remembering)

Yes! *(Turns around, a smile of fascination)* You're English, *aren't* you?

MRS. TOOTHE
(Playing it cool and natural)

British, yes.

JACK

And you lived in London . . . some, some time ago.

MRS. TOOTHE
(Hedging)

Yes, I . . . well, I *have* lived in London, but . . .

JACK
(Very pleased)

I *do* remember you, dear lady. By God, if I were *sober,* I doubt I would. *(Laughs greatly)* Oh yes! Do I remember you!

MRS. TOOTHE
(Playing it through)

You must be mistaken. I never forget faces, and . . .

JACK

Oh, lady; I remember you well, I remember your . . .

(Another fit of laughing) . . . your ladies, I . . . *(Looks about the room, sees the trapped and embarrassed faces, breaks into more laughter)* Oh no! No! Tell me it's not true! It is! It is true! *(More laughter)*

BERYL

I don't know what you're thinking, Jack, but I suspect that you may have had a little too much to drink, and . . .

JACK

Has Madam found herself another group of ladies? *(Laughter as he talks)* Are we operating in the suburbs now? *(Mock commiseration, laughter)* Oh, my poor Beryl! Dear Cynthia! Proud Louise! *(Sees JENNY; his tone now is a cross to disappointment and wonder at the future possibilities)* And oh my darling Jenny!

RICHARD

Stay away from her.

JACK

And all that . . . and all that money lying on the . . . *(Breaks into more laughter)* . . . "Someone sent it to us in the mail?" *(Laughter)* Gentlemen . . . I don't know who arranged all this; but if you guys did, you're better businessmen than I ever thought you were. *(Laughs, starts for french doors)*

MRS. TOOTHE
(Eyes narrowing)

Stop him.

PERRY

Where do you think you're going?

JACK
(Still laughing)

Hm?

PERRY

I said where do you think you're going?

JACK

Why, I thought I'd go back to the cl— *(Breaks down in laughter again)*

MRS. TOOTHE

He'll talk. *(This was a command)*

JENNY

Yes. He will.

MRS. TOOTHE
(Even more clear than before)

He'll talk.
(PERRY grabs JACK by the arm; CHUCK steps in front of him, barring his way)

PERRY

Hold on, old friend.

CHUCK

Easy now.

JACK
(Panic and anger rising)

Let . . . Let me go. God damn it, let me . . .
(He begins to struggle; RICHARD and GILBERT come to the aid of PERRY and CHUCK)

GILBERT

Get him!
> *(They are on him, just restraining at first, but
> the more JACK struggles, the more they are on
> him)*

JACK

Let me . . . Get your hands off me . . . Let! Me! God damn
it! Let! Me!
> *(They have him down, are on top of him)*

PERRY

Hold him! Hold him down!

JACK
> *(Really shouting)*

STOP IT! STOP IT!

MRS. TOOTHE
> *(On her feet, but not in a rush; a commander)*

He's drunk; he'll talk. You must make him be quiet.
> *(JACK continues to struggle, bites CHUCK's hand)*

CHUCK
> *(In rage and reflex, strikes JACK across the face
> with the back of his hand)*

God damn you!

JACK

STOP! IT!

MRS. TOOTHE

Keep him quiet!
> *(RICHARD grabs a pillow from the sofa and,
> together, two or three of them press it over
> JACK's face. His shouts become muffled as they*

*hold the pillow on his face, stiff-armed. Finally
there is silence. The men relax a little, slowly
get off their knees, unwind some, look at* JACK'S
prone, still form; they move about a little)

GILBERT

He's out.

RICHARD
(Grim laugh)

For a while.

MRS. TOOTHE
(Goes over, bends over JACK, *examines him
for a moment, straightens up)*
No. Not for a while. *(Begins to walk back to her chair)*

JENNY
(Pitiful; moves toward JACK)

Jack?

MRS. TOOTHE
(Cruelly casual, but serious)
Don't bother. He's dead.

GILBERT
(Offended)
What do you mean he's dead!

MRS. TOOTHE
Look for your*self*. He's *dead*.

GILBERT
(Looks for himself)
Yes. He is. He's dead.

*(JENNY and CYNTHIA begin to weep, quietly;
LOUISE turns away; the men look at one another)*

BERYL
(Final; catatonic)

Well.

CHUCK

I, I don't think we did that, he . . . We didn't do that.

GILBERT

No, we were just . . .

PERRY

He must have had a heart attack.

JENNY
(Going to him)

Oh, my poor, darling Jack . . .

RICHARD

Stay away from him, Jenny.

CHUCK

What . . . what shall we do?

LOUISE
(Ordering it)

He *can't* be dead; it doesn't happen.

CYNTHIA

He would have talked! It would have been all over town.

JENNY
(Defending JACK)

Who says!?

BERYL

You said, for one.

JENNY
(Furious, and near tears)

I did not! I said . . .

MRS. TOOTHE
(Calm)

You said he would talk. You agreed he would.

GILBERT

No one meant to kill him . . .

PERRY

No, it was . . .

RICHARD
(Grim)

I think I'd better call the police, hunh?

CHUCK
(Nodding)

Yeah, yeah.

GILBERT

Yes; you'd better.

MRS. TOOTHE
(Calm, forceful)

Do you think so?

RICHARD
(Sort of disgusted)

What?

MRS. TOOTHE

Do you think you had better call the police?

RICHARD

There's a *dead* man there!

MRS. TOOTHE

I know; I can see. But what will you tell them? The police.

RICHARD

I'll, I'll tell them . . . we were having a party, and, and Jack came in, and he was drunk, and . . .

MRS. TOOTHE

And so you all smothered him?

RICHARD
(Furious)

No! That he was drunk!

BERYL

. . . he kept on drinking . . .

GILBERT

. . . and he had a heart attack.
(Pause, they look to MRS. TOOTHE)

CHUCK

No?

MRS. TOOTHE

You may call the police, if you want to. *Do* let me leave first, though. I wouldn't want to be listed among those present when the autopsy is done and they find the marks on him and the hemorrhage in the lungs. That happens when people are killed that way, you know; the lungs rupture.

(Silence)

GILBERT

Oh.

(Silence)

PERRY

I see.

(Silence)

BERYL

Well. We can't take *that* chance, can we.
(Silence. JENNY *weeps quietly)*

LOUISE
(Slowly)

No. We can't.

RICHARD
(Quietly loathing)

What do you suggest we do, then?
(They all look to MRS. TOOTHE, *save* JENNY*)*

MRS. TOOTHE
(To RICHARD*)*

I know you think I'm a monster, so . . . if I ask you a question, it won't matter much.

RICHARD
(Waiting)

Yes?

MRS. TOOTHE

What . . . what is the purpose of that deep trench you've
dug near your brick wall?
(Silence)

RICHARD
(Calm response; much underneath)
I've been looking for the cesspool line.

MRS. TOOTHE

Have you found it?

RICHARD
(Still staring at her)
No.

MRS. TOOTHE
(After a pause)
Well, then. Bury him.
*(Silence. The guests look at each other, calmly,
speculatively)*

RICHARD
(Slowly)
You can't mean that.

MRS. TOOTHE
(To all the men)
Go on; bury him.

RICHARD
(Smiling a little)
No.

MRS. TOOTHE

All right, then. Call the police.

(Silence; the men look at one another, slowly, steadily. Then, as if it had all been organized, they slowly move to work. They go to JACK, take him by the legs, arms, under the head, and take him out into the garden, disappear from our sight)

JENNY
(After they have gone; rises, starts after them)
Jack! Richard!

MRS. TOOTHE
Jenny! Come here!
(BERYL and LOUISE go to JENNY, who is help-lessly, quietly crying now, and gently bring her back to the group. They all sit)

JENNY
You . . . they just can't . . . do that.

MRS. TOOTHE
Hush, my dear. Hush.
(This is a wake and the ladies have sorrow on their faces)

LOUISE
(Sincere; helpless)
Poor *Jack*.

BERYL
Yes; poor Jack.

LOUISE
At least it wasn't . . . one of us. I mean, someone, well . . . with a family, someone . . . regular.
(JENNY is quietly hysterical)

MRS. TOOTHE

You haven't put up with death, have you, Jenny?

(JENNY *shakes her head*)

I'm sorry to say you get used to it!

JENNY

N-never!

MRS. TOOTHE

You should have been in London in the war. You would
have learned about death . . . and violence . . . All those
nights in the shelters, with the death going on. Death and
dying. Always take the former if you can.

LOUISE

(Nodding at the sad truth)

Yes.

MRS. TOOTHE

You must help your husbands. You'll have to, I think
. . . for a while. They may wake up at night; sweat; they
may . . . lose heart. You'll have to be the strong ones
. . . as usual.

BERYL

Yes.

MRS. TOOTHE

I wouldn't try to make them go on as if nothing has happened. For something *has* happened . . . very much so.
One of the things that *does* happen . . . one of the ac-
commodations that have to be made. Do you see, Jenny?

JENNY

I don't know.

MRS. TOOTHE
(Sweet; gentle)

You can't go *back*. You have to make do with what is.
And what is leads to what will be. You make the best
as you go on. Like our looks, when we age, as we are
doing, or will. Some of us have our faces lifted, I suppose, and we convince . . . some people—not as many as
we'd like to—but we don't believe it ourselves, do we,
Jenny?

JENNY
(A little girl at lessons)

I shouldn't think so. No.

MRS. TOOTHE

No. We do what will help, which is all we can.

JENNY
(Instructed)

Yes.

*(The men come back in, subdued, clothes a lit-
tle awry, hands dirty)*

GILBERT

All done.

PERRY

Finished.

CHUCK

You'd never know.

RICHARD

. . . unless you had a mind.

CHUCK

Unless you knew.

RICHARD

Yes.
(Goes to JENNY; *in fact, all the men gravitate to their wives)*

CYNTHIA
(Kindly)
Would any of you like a drink? Darling?

PERRY

No; no thanks.

LOUISE

Darling?

GILBERT

Yes. A quick one.

RICHARD
(To JENNY; *comforting)*
You O.K.?

JENNY
(Brave smile)
Sure. You?

RICHARD
(Empty)
Considering.

MRS. TOOTHE

Well; you've all done very well. I think it's time I should be getting on.

BERYL

Yes; well, we all should.

GILBERT

Yes. What time are Don and Betty coming over?

LOUISE

Oh, my God! Eight o'clock. You're right, we've got . . .

CHUCK

Your husband is hungry.

BERYL

Well, all right then, I'll feed you.

MRS. TOOTHE
(To PERRY*)*

I'll call you tomorrow and come to see the house?

PERRY

Yes; fine.

RICHARD

You're all just . . . leaving?

CHUCK
(What else?)

Yes; I think we should.

PERRY

There's nothing we can do, is there?

RICHARD
(Quiet, intense)

There's a body out there; Jack.

GILBERT

It's all *right,* Richard.

PERRY

Really, Richard; it's O.K.

BERYL

Yes, it *is.*

MRS. TOOTHE

Go home, children, it's all right.

CHUCK

Yes, well, I don't know what more we can do.

LOUISE

Yes, we do have Don and Betty coming over.

CYNTHIA

Do you mean Don and Betty Grainger?

LOUISE

Yes.

PERRY

I still can't get over Harry Burns.

GILBERT

Harry Bernstein, you mean.
                    (The guests have gone)

MRS. TOOTHE
(To JENNY *and* RICHARD*)*

The grass will grow over; the earth will be rich, and soon
—eventually—everything in the garden . . . will be as it
was. You'll see.

(MRS. TOOTHE exits, followed by RICHARD and JENNY seeing her out almost by reflex. Bare stage for a moment)
(JACK comes in from the garden, his clothes dirty, sod in his hair)

JACK
(He will speak only to the audience from now on, even when RICHARD and JENNY return; nor will they notice him, of course)

Oh, don't get any ideas, now. I'm dead, believe me. I'm *dead*. It's amazing how dying sobers you up. Well, I certainly never thought it would be *this* way—like this; I'd imagined sliding gently from the bar stool at the club, or crashing into a truck on a curve some night, but never this. Shows you can't tell. God! Would you believe it? Mrs. Toothe, and Beryl and Cynthia and Louise? And poor Jenny? *I* wouldn't have; but, then, I'm rather selfish —self-concerned. *Was*. I must get *used* to that; past tense. Poor Jenny and Richard. They're the only ones I feel badly about—the guilt, and all the rest. That old Madam can take care of herself, and the others . . . who cares? But Jenny and Richard . . . that's a different matter. I *worry* for them.

(JENNY and RICHARD re-enter, move about slowly. JACK puts a finger to his lips, to shush the audience, whether necessary or not)

JENNY
(Timid)

Well.

RICHARD
(Emptied)

Yes.

JENNY
(Trying to be conversational)
Where did you send Roger?

RICHARD
To the club. To swim.

JENNY
(Genuine)
That was nice of you.

RICHARD
Stupid taking it out on him.

JENNY
Yes. *(Pause)* I think we'd better clean up—all the glasses
and everything.

RICHARD
All right.

JACK
*(Watches them for a moment; back to the audi-
ence)*
Here's the *awful* irony of it.

JENNY
(Remembering)
We're to say . . . nothing.

RICHARD
What will happen? He'll have just . . . disappeared?

JENNY
Yes; I guess so.

RICHARD

Roger *brought* him here.

JENNY

Yes, but we'll say Jack just stayed for a little, and then went on.

RICHARD

They'll ask?

JENNY

Someone will; someone's bound to—insurance people, somebody.

RICHARD

We must make a story.

JENNY

Yes. I'll talk to the others.

RICHARD

All right.

JENNY
(So sincere; explaining so much)
Darling . . . I do *love* you.

RICHARD
(Timid)
Yes; and I love you.

JACK

The irony; I was going to tell you the irony. Remember I said I'd made my will over, left it all to Richard and Jenny? Well, it was true; I wasn't kidding. Three and a

half million; every penny, and my house here, *and* in
Nassau. It's all theirs.

JENNY

Let's put the glasses on the tray here.

JACK

Problem now is, they'll have to wait. If I've just . . .
vanished . . . disappeared from the face of the earth, it'll
be seven years until I can be declared officially dead.
And there'll *be* an investigation; you can be sure of that.
I hope they make it stick—the story they tell. I imagine
they will.

RICHARD

What shall I do with the caviar?

JENNY

Give it here; I'll cover it and put it in the fridge.

JACK

But seven years; that's a very long time. So much can
happen. With all they're doing, in seven years their lives
can be ruined. They have so much to live with. (*To*
RICHARD *and* JENNY) You've got to be strong! You've
got to hold on!

JENNY

Darling?

RICHARD

Mmm?

JENNY

I was thinking . . . that house Mrs. Toothe is taking.

RICHARD

What about it?

JENNY

I think it ought to be planted nicely, flowers and shrubs and all. Make it look like it's really lived in. It mustn't look like it's been let go. It might draw suspicion. You notice things like that.

RICHARD

Yes; you do.

JENNY

Gardens that have been let go. If people let them go, you know there's something wrong in the house.

RICHARD

Yes.

JENNY

I think it should be well planted and taken care of; kept up. I think it should look like all the others. Don't you think so?

RICHARD
(Straight)

Yes; I think you're right.

JACK

Well . . . I think they'll make it.

CURTAIN

DO YOU REALLY UNDERSTAND YOUR CHILD?

A PRIMER
FOR PARENTS
by Dr. Jerome S. Fass

What is he saying

...when he sucks his thumb?
..when he doesn't want to go to school?
...when he bites his nails?
...when he does something he's been told not to?
...when he fights with other children in the family?

Often, a child's actions are messages...appeals for love, help, or understanding...if only we could "read" them. Now, here is the book that shows you how.

Partial listing of contents:

- Instant Einstein
- Sloppy sleepers
- Birds, bees and parents too
- Threatening habits
- Smotherly love
- Discipline and communication
- Toiling in the toilet
- Goodbye mama, goodbye papa
- Whining and dining

MAIL THIS COUPON NOW—FOR FREE 10-DAY TRIAL

TRIDENT PRESS DEPT. TP-10
630 Fifth Avenue, New York, New York 10020

Please rush me .... copy(ies) of A PRIMER FOR PARENTS to read for 10 days free. I must be completely satisfied or I may return it within 10 days and owe nothing. Otherwise I will send only $4.95, plus mailing costs, as payment in full.

Name...
(please print)
Address...

City.......................State.......................Zip...................

☐ **Save postage.** Check here if you enclose check or money order for $4.95 as payment in full—then we pay postage. Same 10-day trial privilege with full refund guarantee holds.

77063